WITHDRAWN

NADJA

BY ANDRÉ BRETON

TRANSLATED BY RICHARD HOWARD

GROVE PRESS, INC. / NEW YORK

LIST OF ILLUSTRATIONS

5

*W*ho am I? If this once I were to rely on a proverb, then perhaps everything would amount to knowing whom I "haunt." I must admit that this last word is misleading, tending to establish between certain beings and myself relations that are stranger, more inescapable, more disturbing than I intended. Such a word means much more than it says, makes me, still alive, play a ghostly part, evidently referring to what I must have ceased to be in order to be *who* I am. Hardly distorted in this sense, the word suggests that what I regard as the objective, more or less deliberate manifestations of my existence are merely the premises, within the limits of this existence, of an activity whose true extent is quite unknown to me. My image of the "ghost," including everything conventional about its appearance as well as its blind submission to certain contingencies of time and place, is particularly significant for me as the finite representation of a torment that may be eternal. Perhaps my life is nothing but an image of this kind; perhaps I am doomed to retrace my steps under the illusion that I am exploring, doomed to try and learn what I should simply recognize, learning a mere fraction of what I have forgotten. This sense of myself seems inadequate only insofar as it *presupposes* myself, arbitrarily preferring a completed image of my mind which need not be reconciled with time, and insofar as it implies—within this same time—an idea of irreparable loss, of punishment, of a fall whose lack of moral basis is, as I see it, indisputable. What matters is that the particular aptitudes my day-to-day life gradually reveals should not distract me from my search for a general aptitude which would be peculiar to me and which is not innate. Over and above the various prejudices I acknowledge, the affinities I feel, the attractions I succumb to, the events which occur to me and to me alone—over and above a sum of movements I am conscious of making, of emotions I alone experience—I strive, in relation to other men, to discover the nature, if not the necessity, of my difference from them. Is it not precisely to the degree I become conscious of this difference that I shall recognize what I alone have been put on this earth to do, what unique message I alone may bear, so that I alone can answer for its fate?

Such reflections lead me to the conclusion that criticism, abjuring, it is true, its dearest prerogatives but aiming, on the whole, at a goal less futile than the automatic adjustment of ideas, should confine itself to scholarly incursions upon the very realm supposedly barred to it, and which, separate from the work, is a realm where the author's personality, victimized by the petty events of daily life, expresses itself quite freely and often in so distinctive a manner. Consider this anecdote: Hugo, toward the end of his life, took the same ride with Juliette Drouet every day, always interrupting his wordless meditation when their carriage passed an estate with two gates, one large, one small; pointing to the large gate, Hugo, for perhaps the thousandth time, would say: "Bridle gate, Madame," to which Juliette, pointing to the small gate, would reply: "Pedestrian gate, Monsieur"; then, a little farther on, passing two trees with intertwining branches, Hugo would remark: "Philemon and Baucis," knowing that Juliette would

not answer; we have reason to believe that this marvelous, poignant ritual was repeated daily for years
on end; yet how could the best possible study of
Hugo's work give us a comparable awareness, the
astonishing sense of what he was, of what he is?
Those two gates are like the mirror of his strength
and his weakness, we do not know which stands for
his insignificance, which for his greatness. And what
good would all the genius in the world be to us if
it failed to countenance that adorable correction, the
redress of love itself, which so perfectly characterizes
Juliette's reply? The subtlest, the most enthusiastic
of Hugo's critics will never make me feel anything
to equal this supreme sense of *proportion*. I should
be privileged indeed to possess, in the case of each
of the men I admire, a personal document of corresponding value. Lacking these, I should even be
content with records of a lesser value, less self-con-
tained from an emotional point of view. I do not
admire Flaubert, yet when I am told that by his own
admission all he hoped to accomplish in *Salammbô*
was to "give the impression of the color yellow,"
and in *Madame Bovary* "to do something that would
have the color of those mouldy cornices that harbor
wood lice," and that he cared for nothing else, such
generally extra-literary preoccupations leave me anything but indifferent. The magnificent light in Cour-
bet's paintings is for me the same as that of the Place

Vendôme, at the time the Column fell. If today a man like Chirico would confide—entirely and, of course, artlessly, including the least consequential as well as the most disturbing details—what it was that once made him paint as he did, such a step, taken by such a man, would mean an enormous advance for exegesis. Without him, indeed despite him, merely by means of his early paintings and a manuscript notebook before me as I write, we can only imperfectly reconstruct his universe up till 1917. How deeply I regret my inability to fill this gap, to grasp all that contradicts the natural order in such a universe, creating a new scale of things. Chirico acknowledged at the time that he could paint only when *surprised* (surprised first of all) by certain arrangements of objects, and that the entire enigma of revelation consisted for him in this word: surprise. Certainly the resulting work remained "closely linked with what had provoked its birth," but resembled it only "in the strange way two brothers resemble each other, or rather as a dream about someone resembles that person in reality. It is, and at the same time is not, the same person; a slight and mysterious transfiguration is apparent in the features." Without considering the actual arrangements of objects which for Chirico exhibit a flagrant peculiarity, critical attention may still turn to these objects themselves and determine why it is always these same ones, in such

small numbers, that are called upon to arrange themselves in this way. We have said nothing about
Chirico until we take into account his most personal
views about the artichoke, the glove, the cookie, or
the spool. In such matters as these, how much we
could gain from his co-operation! As far as I am
concerned, a mind's arrangement with regard to certain objects is even more important than its regard
for certain arrangements of objects, these two kinds
of arrangement controlling between them all forms
of sensibility. Thus with Huysmans, the Huysmans
of *En Rade* and *Là-Bas*, I find so much in common
about our ways of valuing the world, of choosing
with all the partiality of despair among what exists,
that though unfortunately I have been unable to
know him save by his work, he is, perhaps, less of
a stranger to me than any of my friends. But has
he not also done more than anyone else to consum-
mate that necessary, *vital* discrimination between the
apparently fragile link which can be of the utmost
aid to us and the dizzying array of forces which
conspire together for our destruction? He has fa-
miliarized me with that tremulous ennui which almost any spectacle induced in him; no one before
Huysmans could, if not exemplify this great victory
of the involuntary over the ravaged domain of conscious possibilities, at least convince me in human
terms of its absolute inevitability and of the use-

lessness of trying to find loopholes for myself. How grateful I am to him for letting me know, without caring about the effect such revelations produced, everything that affects him, that occupies him in his hours of gravest anxiety, everything external to his anxiety, for not pathetically "singing" his distress like too many poets, but for enumerating patiently, in the darkness, some quite involuntary reasons he still found for being, and for being—to whose advantage he never really knew—a writer! He, too, is the object of one of those perpetual solicitations which seem to come from beyond, which momentarily possess us before one of those chance arrangements, of a more or less unfamiliar character, whose secret we feel might be learned merely by questioning ourselves closely enough. Need I add how differently I regard Huysmans from all those empiricists of the novel who claim to give us characters separate from themselves, to define them physically, morally—in their fashion!—in the service of some cause we should prefer to disregard! Out of one real character about whom they suppose they know something they make two characters in their story; out of two, they make one. And we even bother to argue! Someone suggested to an author I know, in connection with a work of his about to be published and whose heroine might be too readily recognized, that he change at least the color of her hair. As a blonde, apparently, she might have avoided betraying a brunette. I do not regard such a thing as childish, I regard it as monstrous. I insist on knowing the names, on being interested only in books left ajar, like doors; I will not go looking for keys. Happily the days of psychological literature, with all its fictitious plots, are numbered. And there is no doubt that the mortal blow was delivered by Huysmans. I myself shall continue living in my glass house where you can always see who comes to call; where everything hanging from the ceiling and on the walls stays where it is as if by magic, where I sleep nights in a glass bed, under glass sheets, where *who I am* will sooner or later appear etched by a diamond. Certainly nothing in this regard distresses me so much as Lautréamont's complete disappearance behind his work, and his terrible "tics, tics, and tics" is constantly in my thoughts. But I find something supernatural in the circumstances of a human obliteration so complete. It would be only too futile to aspire to it, and I readily persuade myself that such a wish on the part of those who take shelter behind it indicates the kind of ambition that is scarcely honorable. Monsieur Tristan Tzara would doubtless prefer it not to be known that during the performance of the *Coeur à Barbe* in Paris he handed us—Paul Eluard and myself—over to the police, though a spontaneous action of this sort is so profoundly revealing that in its light, which cannot help being that of history as well, Tzara's *25 Poems* (the title of one of his books) becomes *25 Policeman's Lucubrations.*

I intend to mention, in the margin of the narrative I have yet to relate, only the most decisive episodes of my life *as I can conceive it apart from its organic plan,* and only insofar as it is at the mercy of chance —the merest as well as the greatest—temporarily escaping my control, admitting me to an almost forbidden world of sudden parallels, petrifying coincidences, and reflexes peculiar to each individual, of harmonies struck as though on the piano, flashes of light that would make you see, really *see,* if only they were not so much quicker than all the rest. I am concerned with facts of quite unverifiable intrinsic value, but which, by their absolutely unexpected, violently fortuitous character, and the kind of associations of suspect ideas they provoke—a way of transforming gossamer into spiderweb (that is, into what would be the most shimmering, delicate thing in the world were it not for the spider in the corner); I am concerned, I say, with facts which may belong to the order of pure observation, but which on each occasion present all the appearances of a signal, without our being able to say precisely which signal, and of what; facts which when I am alone permit me to enjoy unlikely complicities, which convince me of my error in occasionally presuming I stand at the helm alone. Such facts, from the simplest to the most complex, should be assigned a hierarchy, from the special, indefinable reaction at the sight of extremely rare objects or upon our arrival in a strange place (both accompanied by the distinct sensation that something momentous, something essential depends upon them), to the complete lack of peace with ourselves provoked by certain juxtapositions, certain combinations of circumstances which greatly surpass our understanding and permit us to resume rational activity only if, in most cases, we call upon our very instinct of self-preservation to enable us to do so. We might establish a number of intermediate steps between such slope-facts and such cliff-facts. Between those of which I can be only the agonized witness and those others about which I flatter myself I possess the full details, there is perhaps the same distance as between one of those declarations or series of declarations which constitutes the sentence or the text known as "surrealist" and the declaration or series of declarations which, for the same observer, constitutes the sentence or the text whose every term he has fully weighed and measured. He does not consider his responsibility involved, so to speak, in the first case; it is involved in the second. On the other hand, he is infinitely more surprised, more fascinated by what happens in the former than in the latter. He is also prouder of

PLATE I. My point of departure will be
the Hôtel des Grands Hommes . . .

(SEE PAGE 23)

PLATE 2. The Manoir d'Ango
in Varengeville-sur-Mer
(SEE PAGE 23)

it, which is certainly remarkable, and feels the freer for it. This is the case with those privileged sensations I have mentioned and whose share of incommunicability is itself a source of pleasures that have no equal.

Do not expect me to provide an exact account of what I have been permitted to experience in this domain. I shall limit myself here to recalling without effort certain things which, apart from any exertions on my part, have occasionally happened to me, things which, reaching me in unsuspected ways, give me the measure of the particular grace and disgrace of which I am the object; I shall discuss these things without pre-established order, and according to the mood of the moment which lets whatever survives survive. My point of departure will be the Hôtel des Grands Hommes, Place du Panthéon, where I lived around 1918, and my first halt the Manoir d'Ango in Varengeville-sur-Mer, where I stayed in August, 1927, still very much the same person—the Manoir d'Ango where I was offered the hospitality, when I wished to be undisturbed, of a hut artificially camouflaged by shrubbery, at the edge of a woods; here, while in other respects occupying myself with whatever I liked, I was able to hunt owls as well. (Could it have been otherwise, once I decided to write *Nadja*?) Actually, it is of little importance if an occasional error or omission, a genuine anomaly or lacuna casts a shadow across my narrative, across what, taken as a whole, cannot be substantiated. I must insist, lastly, that such accidents of thought not be reduced to their *unjust* proportion as *faits-divers*, random episodes, so that when I say, for instance, that the statue of Etienne Dolet on its plinth in the Place Maubert in Paris has always fascinated me and induced unbearable discomfort, it will not immediately be supposed that I am merely ready for psychoanalysis, a method I respect and whose present aims I consider nothing less than the expulsion of man from himself, and of which I expect other exploits than those of a bouncer. I am convinced, moreover, that as a discipline psychoanalysis is not qualified to deal with such phenomena, since despite its great merits we already do this method too much honor by conceding that it exhausts the problem of dreams or that it does not simply occasion further inhibitions by its very interpretation of inhibitions. Which leads me to my own experience, to what is for me, concerning myself, a virtually continuous subject of meditation and reverie:

The day of the first performance of Apollinaire's *Couleur du Temps* at the Conservatoire Renée Maubel, while I was talking to Picasso in the balcony during the intermission, a young man approaches me, stammers a few words, and finally manages to ex-

PLATE 3. When I say that the statue of Etienne Dolet on its plinth
in the Place Maubert in Paris has always fascinated me
and induced unbearable discomfort . . .

(SEE PAGE 24)

PHOTO: MAN RAY

PLATE 4. Paul Eluard

(SEE PAGE 27)

plain that he had mistaken me for one of his friends supposedly killed in the war. Naturally, nothing more was said. A few days later, through a mutual friend, I begin corresponding with Paul Eluard, whom I did not know by sight. On furlough, he comes to see me: I am in the presence of the same person as at *Couleur du Temps*.

The words BOIS-CHARBONS, which appear on the last page of *Les Champs Magnétiques*, enabled me, during the whole of one Sunday I spent walking with Philippe Soupault, to exhibit a peculiar talent for detecting every shop they serve to designate. It seems to me I was able to say, no matter what street we were in, how far along on the right or left these shops would appear. And my predictions always turned out to be right. I was informed, guided, not by the hallucinatory image of the words in question, but rather by one of those logs in cross-section, crudely painted on the façade, in little piles on each side of the door, all the same color with a darker center. Once I reached home, this image continued to obsess me. A tune from the carousel in the Carrefour Médicis seemed to be this log too. And, from my window, the skull of Jean-Jacques Rousseau as well, whose statue I could see from behind and two or three stories below me. That day I was very frightened.

Still in my hotel, Place du Panthéon, one evening, late. Someone knocks. In comes a woman whose approximate age and features I cannot now recall. In mourning, I think. She asks me for a number of the review *Littérature* which has not yet appeared and which someone has made her promise to take to Nantes the next day. She insists, reluctant though I am, upon having it. But her chief reason for coming, it seems, is to "recommend" the person who has sent her and who will soon be living in Paris. (I still remember the expression "would like to launch himself in literature" which subsequently, knowing to whom it referred, seemed so curious, so moving.) But who was I being urged in this more than chimerical way to welcome, to advise? A few days later, Benjamin Péret was there.

Nantes: perhaps, with Paris, the only city in France where I feel that something worth while can happen to me, where certain eyes burn all too brightly for their own sake (I noticed this only last year, the time it took to cross Nantes by car and see that woman—a workingwoman, I think, accompanied by a man—raise her eyes: I should have stopped), where for me the rhythm of life is not

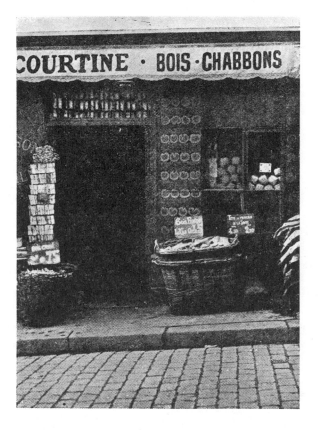

PLATE 5. The words BOIS-CHARBONS

(SEE PAGE 27)

PHOTO: MAN RAY

PLATE 6. A few days later, Benjamin Péret was there

(SEE PAGE 28)

the same as elsewhere, where certain beings still nour-ish a spirit of supreme adventure, Nantes, a city friends can still come to me from, Nantes, where I loved one park: Le parc de Procé.

Once again, now, I see Robert Desnos at the period those of us who knew him call the "Nap Period." He "dozes" but he writes, he talks. It is evening, in my studio over the Cabaret du Ciel. Outside, some-one is shouting: "Come one, come all, come to the Chat Noir!" And Desnos continues seeing what I do not see, what I see only after he shows it to me. He borrows the personality of the most singular man alive as well as the most elusive, the most deceptive, the author of *Le Cimetière des Uniformes et Livrées*, Marcel Duchamp. Desnos has never seen him in real life. What in Duchamp seemed most inimitable through some mysterious "plays on words" (Rrose Sélavy) can be found in Desnos in all its purity and suddenly assumes an extraordinary resonance. Those who have not seen his pencil set on paper—without the slightest hesitation and with an astonishing speed —those amazing poetic equations, and have not ascer-tained, as I have, that they could not have been pre-pared a long time before, even if they are capable of appreciating their technical perfection and of judg-ing their wonderful loftiness, cannot conceive of everything involved in their creation at the time, of the absolutely oracular value they assumed. Someone who was present at those innumerable sessions would have to take the trouble to recount them dispassionately, to describe them precisely, to situate them in their true atmosphere. A discussion of this point is actually called for. Of all the subsequent appointments Desnos, his eyes closed, made for me with himself, with someone else, or with myself, there is not one I feel, even now, I have the heart to miss, not one, at the most unlikely place and time, where I am not sure of finding whomever he has told me about.

Meanwhile, you can be sure of meeting me in Paris, of not spending more than three days without seeing me pass, toward the end of the afternoon, along the Boulevard Bonne-Nouvelle between the *Matin* printing office and the Boulevard de Strasbourg. I don't know why it should be precisely here that my feet take me, here that I almost invariably go without specific purpose, without anything to induce me but this obscure clue: namely that it (?) will happen here. I cannot see, as I hurry along, what could constitute for me, even without my knowing it, a magnetic pole in either space or time. No: not even the extremely handsome, extremely useless Porte Saint-Denis. Not even the memory of the eighth and last episode of a film I saw in the neighborhood, in which a Chinese who had found some way to multiply himself in-

PLATE 7. Once again, now, I see Robert Desnos . . .
(SEE PAGE 31)

PLATE 8. No: not even the extremely handsome, extremely useless Porte Saint-Denis . . .

(SEE PAGE 32)

PLATE 9. This film, which has affected me
far more than any other . . .

(SEE PAGE 37)

L. MAZEAU

COMÉDIES, REVUES, OPÉRETTES

Tours de Chants, Comique Typique

ACTUELLEMENT

Tournée Baret

libre le 6 janvier 1927

RÉFÉRENCES

PARIS

OLYMPIA
CHATELET
SCALA
DEJAZET
CLUNY
TH. MONCEY
TH. NOUVEAU
TH. MODERNE
TH. ALEXANDRETTE
TH. LYRIQUE DU 16

LA FOURMI
VARIETES PARISIENNES
FOLIES PARISIENNES
SUCCES PALACE
CASINO du PONT Charenton
Etc., Etc.

ADRESSE PERMANENTE
124 Rue de Crimée

St Martin le 19 Octobre 1927

Monsieur

Excusez moi si je réponds un peu tardivement à votre lettre du 1er octobre mais étant actuellement en tournée Baret elle n'est venue me rejoindre qu'à Grenoble le 6.

D'autre part les renseignements que je pourrais vous fournir sur le Théâtre Moderne dont je dois avoir quelques photos de [illegible] de Revues, chez moi ne concordent pas avec la [illegible] de cet établissement car j'en faisais partie en 1916 sous direction

PLATE 10. Speaking of the Théâtre Moderne

(SEE PAGE 38)

vaded New York by means of several million self-reproductions. He entered President Wilson's office followed by himself, and by himself, and by himself, and by himself; the President removed his *pince-nez.* This film, which has affected me far more than any other, was called *The Grip of the Octopus.*

With this system which consists, before going into a movie theater, of never looking to see what's playing—which, moreover, would scarcely do me any good, since I cannot remember the names of more than five or six actors—I obviously run the risk of missing more than others, though here I must confess my weakness for the most absolutely absurd French films. I understand, moreover, quite poorly, I *follow* too vaguely. Sometimes this does bother me, and then I question those sitting near me. Nevertheless, certain movie theaters in the tenth arrondissement seem to me to be places particularly intended for me, as during the period when, with Jacques Vaché we would settle down to dinner in the orchestra of the former Théâtre des Folies-Dramatiques, opening cans, slicing bread, uncorking bottles, and talking in ordinary tones, as if around a table, to the great amazement of the spectators, who dared not say a word.

Located at the end of the now destroyed Passage

de l'Opéra, the "Théâtre Moderne," aside from the fact that the plays put on there had still less importance, corresponded perfectly to my ideal in this direction. The ridiculous acting of the performers, who paid only the faintest attention to their parts, scarcely listening to each other and busy making dates with members of the audience, which consisted of perhaps fifteen people at the most, always reminded me of a canvas backdrop. But what could I find for the fleeting and so easily alarmed image of myself, that image I am talking about, which is worth the welcome of this hall with its great, worn mirrors, decorated toward the base with gray swans gliding among yellow reeds, with its grillwork loges entirely without air or light, as suspicious-looking as the hall itself where during the performance rats crept about, running over your feet, where, once inside, you had your choice between a staved-in chair and one that might tip over at any moment! And between the first act and the second—for it was too preposterous to wait for the third—what would I ever see again with these eyes which have seen the "bar" upstairs, terribly dark too with its impenetrable bowers, "a living room at the bottom of a lake," yes really? By coming back here so often, I managed, at the price of so many horrors, the worst imaginable, to memorize one absolutely pure quatrain. It was a woman, oddly enough a pretty one, who sang:

La maison de mon coeur est prête
Et ne s'ouvre qu'à l'avenir.
Puisqu'il n'est rien que je regrette,
Mon bel époux, tu peux venir.*

I have always, beyond belief, hoped to meet, at night and in a woods, a beautiful naked woman or rather, since such a wish once expressed means nothing, I regret, beyond belief, not having met her. Imagining such an encounter is not, after all, so fantastic: it might happen. It seems to me that everything would have stopped short—I would not even be writing what I am writing. I adore this situation which of all situations is the one where I am most likely to have lacked *presence of mind*. I would probably not even have thought of running away. (Anyone who laughs at this last sentence is a pig.) At the end of one afternoon, last year, in the side aisles of the "Electric-Palace," a naked woman, who must have come in wearing only her coat, strolled, dead white, from one row to the next. This in itself was upsetting. Far, unfortunately, from being extraordinary enough, since this section of the "Electric" was the most commonplace sort of illicit sexual rendezvous.

But for me to descend into what is truly the

---

* Var.: *Amour nouveau, tu peux venir.*

mind's lower depths, where it is no longer a question of the night's falling and rising again (and is that the day?), means to follow the Rue Fontaine back to the Théâtre des Deux Masques, which has now been replaced by a cabaret. I once went there, though I have never been able to tolerate the theater, supposing that the play being put on couldn't be bad, so harsh—to the point of demanding that the play be banned—had the criticism of it been. Among the "Grand Guignol" sort of plays customarily constituting the theater's repertory, it had seemed drastically out of place. It will be agreed that this in itself was no ordinary recommendation. I will no longer postpone expressing the unbounded admiration I felt for *Les Détraquées*, which remains and will long remain the only dramatic work (I mean: created exclusively for the stage) which I choose to recall. The play, I insist—and this is not one of its least curious aspects—loses almost everything, or at least every character conflict, by not been *seen*, by not being acted out. With these reservations, I do not consider it unprofitable in other respects to relate its plot.

The curtain rises on the office of the principal of a girls' school. This woman, a rather stout blonde of about forty, is discovered alone and gives signs of great nervous tension. It is the day before vacation, and she is anxiously expecting someone. "Solange should be here by now. . . ." She walks feverishly around the room, touching the furniture, the papers on her desk. From time to time she goes to the window overlooking the garden where we can tell that the recess period has just begun: we have heard the bell, then the occasional happy cries of girls immediately fading into the general racket. A moronic gardener, jerking his head, stammering unendurably, and making terrible mistakes in pronunciation—the boarding-school gardener—is now standing near the door, mumbling vaguely and apparently unwilling to leave. He has come back from the station: Mademoiselle Solange did not get off the train. "Mad-moisell So-lang . . ." He drags the syllables like down-at-the-heel shoes. We too become impatient. However, an elderly woman who has just sent up her card is shown in. She has received a rather confused letter from her granddaughter begging to be taken away at once. The woman lets herself be reassured easily: at this time of year the children are all a little nervous. Besides she need only call the little girl in to ask her if she has anyone or anything to complain about. Here she is. She kisses her grandmother. Soon we see that her eyes can no longer leave those of the woman interrogating her. She makes only a few gestures of denial. Why not wait for the distribution of prizes which is to take place in a few days? We sense that she dare not speak. She will stay at school. The child, abashed, heads for the door. On the threshold, she seems to be torn by a great inner conflict. She exits running. The grandmother, thanking the principal, says goodbye. Again the latter is alone. Again begins the ridiculous, terrible waiting, in which we do not know which object to move, which gesture to repeat—what to do in order to make what we are waiting for happen. . . . At last the sound of a carriage. . . . The principal's face brightens. Confronting eternity. A charming woman enters without knocking. It is she. She casually pushes away the arms which embrace her. Dark, with brown hair, I don't recall. Young. Magnificent eyes that mingle languor with subtlety, cruelty, despair. Slender, dressed in dark colors, black silk stockings. And something *déclassé* about her that is sympathetic. There is no explanation of her presence, though she apologizes for being delayed. Her apparent coldness is in extreme contrast with the welcome given her. She speaks, with a rather affected indifference, of what her life has been—insignificant since the year before, when she was also here, at this same time of year. Without giving any details about the school where she teaches. But (*here the conversation will assume a much more intimate turn*) there is now some question of the friendship Solange has managed to form with some of her more charming, more attractive, more gifted students. She grows reflective. We strain to catch her

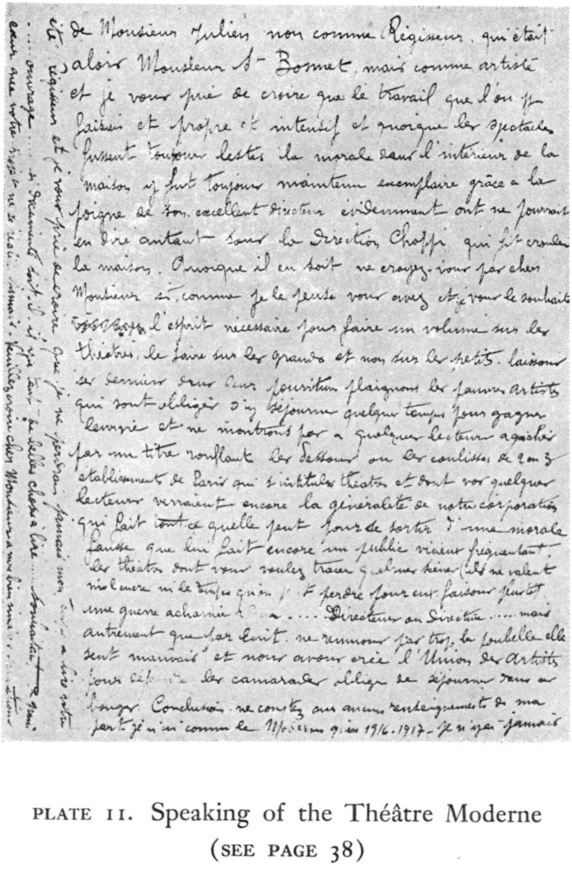
de Monsieur Julien non comme Régisseur, qui était
alors Monsieur St-Bonnet, mais comme artiste
et je vous prie de croire que le travail que l'on y
faisait et propre et intensif et quoique les spectacles
fussent toujours lestes la morale dans l'intérieur de la
maison y fut toujours maintenu exemplaire grâce a la
poigne de son excellent directeur évidemment ont ne pourrait
en dire autant sous la direction Chopp qui fit crouler
la maison. Quoique il en soit ne croyez-vous pas cher
Monsieur si, comme je le pense vous avez et je vous le souhaite
~~vous~~ l'esprit nécessaire pour faire un volume sur les
théatres, le faire sur les grands et non sur les petits. laissons
ces derniers dans leur pourriture plaignons les pauvres artistes
qui sont obligés d'y séjourner quelque temps pour gagner
leur vie et ne montrons pas a quelques lecteurs aguichés
par un titre ronflant les dessous ou les coulisses de 2 ou 3
établissements de Paris qui s'intitulent théatres et dont vos quelques
lecteurs verraient encore la généralité de notre corporation
qui fait tout ce quelle peut pour se sortir d'une morale
fausse que lui fait encore un public vicieux fréquentant
les théatres dont vous voulez tracer quelques scènes (ils ne valent
ni l'encre ni le temps qu'on peut perdre pour eux faisons plutot
une guerre acharnée à ces.... Directeurs ou Directrices..... mais
autrement que par écrit. ne remuons pas trop la poubelle elle
sent mauvais et nous avons créé l'Union des Artistes
pour défendre les camarades obligés de séjourner dans ce
bouge. Conclusion ne comptez sur aucuns renseignements de ma
part. je n'ai connu le Mosserno (?) qu'en 1916-1917 - Je n'y ai jamais

PLATE 11. Speaking of the Théâtre Moderne

(SEE PAGE 38)

PLATE 12. The child of a moment ago
enters without a word . . .
(SEE PAGE 45)

words as they escape her lips. Suddenly she breaks off, we have just time enough to see her open her bag, raise her skirt revealing a beautiful leg and there, a little above the black garter. . . . "But you didn't give yourself a fix!" "No, oh now, what do you expect." This answer made in a tone of such poignant lassitude. As though revived, Solange asks for information in her turn: "And what about you . . . here? Tell me." Here too there have been such nice *new* students. One in particular. So sweet. "Dear, wait a moment." The two women lean out of the window for a long moment. Silence. A BALLOON FALLS IN THE ROOM. Silence. "There she is! She's coming up." "Do you think so?" Both are leaning against the wall. Solange closes her eyes, relaxes, sighs, stands motionless. Someone knocks. The child of a moment ago enters without a word, slowly approaches the balloon, her eyes fixed on the principal's; she walks on tiptoe. Curtain. —The next act opens at night, in an anteroom. Several hours have passed. A doctor, with his black bag. A child has disappeared. Everyone hopes nothing serious has happened to her. The house and garden have been searched from top to bottom. The principal enters, calmer than before. "An extremely sweet child, perhaps a little sad. Heavens, and her grandmother was here only a few hours ago! I've just sent for her." The doctor is suspicious: for two consecutive years there has been an accident just when the children are leaving. Last year a body was discovered in the well. This year . . . Enter the prophetic, bleating gardener. He has gone to look down the well. "It's queer, that's what it is, downright queer." The doctor vainly questions the gardener. "It's queer." He has searched the whole garden with a lantern. Impossible for the girl to have left. The gates are locked. The walls are high. And there is no sign of her in the house. The gardener continues arguing with himself, hashing over the same evidence in a less and less intelligible manner. The doctor is no longer listening. "It's queer. The year before. I didn't see a thing. I'll have to put a candle in tomorrow. . . . Where can that little girl be? M'sieur le docteur. All right, M'sieur le docteur. Still, it's queer. . . . And didn't Ma-moisell-So-lange come yesterday, just like that. . . ."—"Did you say Mademoiselle Solange was here? Are you sure? (It's more like last year than I thought.) All right, that's all." The doctor hides behind a column. It is not yet daylight. Solange crosses the stage. She does not appear to share the general emotion, she walks straight ahead, like an automaton. —A short while later. All the searching has proved vain. We are again in the principal's office. The child's grandmother has just been taken ill in the parlor. She must be given medical attention at once. Certainly both these women seem to have

PHOTO: HENRI MANUEL

PLATE 13. Blanche Derval

(SEE PAGE 49)

clear consciences. We consider the doctor. The inspector. The servants. Solange. The principal. . . . The latter, looking for a cordial, goes to the first-aid cabinet, opens it. The child's bloody corpse appears, head downward, and falls onto the floor. The scream, the unforgettable scream. (In the performance, it was considered advisable to inform the audience that the actor playing the child was over seventeen. The important thing is that she seemed about eleven.) I don't know whether the scream I refer to brought the play to an end, but I hope that its authors (the play was the result of a collaboration between the comic actor Palau and, I believe, a surgeon named Thierry, but must have had the assistance of some demon as well) did not expect Solange to endure anything more; this character, too alluring to be true, should never be obliged to submit to a show of punishment which, moreover, she denied with all her splendor. I shall merely add that the role was played by the most admirable and probably the *only* actress of the period, whose work I saw at the Deux Masques in several other plays where she was no less beautiful, but of whom, perhaps to my great disgrace, I have never heard anyone speak: Blanche Derval.

(As I was finishing the above account last evening, I abandoned myself once more to the conjectures that become unavoidable whenever I see this play again—some three or four times, now—or whenever

I run through it in my own mind. The lack of adequate indications as to what happens after the balloon falls and the ambiguity about precisely what Solange and her partner are a prey to that transforms them into these magnificent predatory beasts is still what puzzles me *par excellence*. As I woke this morning, I had unusual difficulty shaking off a rather squalid dream which I feel no need to transcribe here, since it derives chiefly from conversations I had yesterday and bears no relation to this subject. This dream seems interesting only insofar as it is symptomatic of the repercussion such recollections, provided one surrenders to them with a certain violence, may have on the course of one's thought. It is remarkable, first of all, that the dream in question emphasized only the painful, repugnant, not to say cruel aspect of the considerations I had embarked upon, that it scrupulously suppressed everything I regard as their fabulous value, like an extract of amber or an ageless attar of roses. On the other hand, I must admit that if I wake, seeing quite clearly what has just occurred: a moss-colored insect about twenty inches long, taking the place of an old man, has just headed toward some kind of machine, slipped one penny into the slot instead of two, which seemed to me to constitute a particularly reprehensible fraud, to such a degree that, as though inadvertently, I struck it with my cane and felt it fall on my head—

I had time to notice its eyeballs gleam on my hat-brim before I choked and it was with only the greatest difficulty that two of its huge hairy legs were removed from my throat while I experienced an inexpressible disgust—it is clear that on the surface, this dream *primarily* relates to the fact that on the ceiling of the loggia where I have been sitting the last few days there is a nest around which flutters a bird which my presence rather alarms each time it brings back from the fields, chirping as it flies, something like a big green grasshopper. But it is indisputable that the transposition, the intense fixation, the otherwise inexplicable passage of such an image from the level of a banal remark to the emotive level, necessarily includes a reference to certain episodes of *Les Detraquées* and the reversion to those conjectures I was speaking of. Since the production of dream images always depends on at least this *double play of mirrors*, there is, here, the indication of the highly special, supremely revealing, "super-determinant"—in the Freudian sense of the word—role which certain powerful impressions are made to play, in no way contaminable by morality, actually experienced "beyond good and evil" in the dream, and, subsequently, in what we quite arbitrarily oppose to dream under the name of reality.)

The extremely deep and vivid emotion which the

reading of Rimbaud gave me around 1915 and which, of his entire work, only a very few poems such as *Dévotion* continue to provide, is doubtless, at this period, what enabled me, one day in the country, when I was out walking alone in a downpour, to meet a girl who turned to me without any warning, as I was walking along beside her, and asked my permission to recite one of her favorite poems: Rimbaud's *Dormeur du Val.* This was quite unexpected, quite improbable. Again quite recently, when Marcel Noll and I went one Sunday to the Saint-Ouen flea-market (I go there often, searching for objects that can be found nowhere else: old-fashioned, broken, useless, almost incomprehensible, even perverse—at least in the sense I give to the word and which I prefer—like, for example, that kind of irregular, white, shellacked half-cylinder covered with reliefs and depressions that are meaningless to me, streaked with horizontal and vertical reds and greens, preciously nestled in a case under a legend in Italian, which I brought home and which after careful examination I have finally identified as some kind of statistical device, operating three-dimensionally and recording the population of a city in such and such a year, though all this makes it no more comprehensible to me), our attention was simultaneously caught by a brand new copy of Rimbaud's *Oeuvres Complètes* lost in a tiny, wretched bin of rags, yellowed

PLATE 14. When I went one Sunday
to the Saint-Ouen flea-market
(SEE PAGE 52)

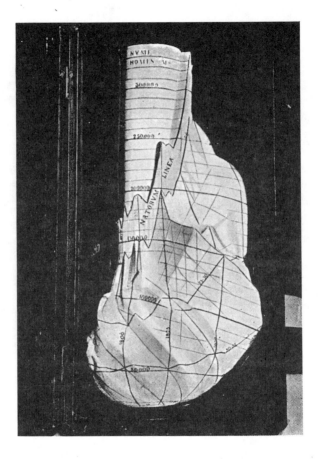

PLATE 15. Even perverse, like that kind of
irregular white half-cylinder . . .

(SEE PAGE 52)

nineteenth-century photographs, worthless books, and iron spoons. Fortunately I decide to leaf through this volume, for I have time to discover there two sheets of paper stuck between the pages: one a type-written copy of a poem in free verse, the other a penciled series of reflections on Nietzsche. But the saleswoman leaves me no time to learn more. The volume is not for sale, the documents it contains belong to her. She is still a young woman and extremely jovial. She continues speaking with a great deal of animation to someone who seems to be a workman of her acquaintance and who listens to her, apparently, with delight. We too engage her in conversation. Extremely cultivated, she has no objection to discussing her literary favorites which are: Shelley, Nietzsche, and Rimbaud. Quite spontaneously she even mentions the surrealists and Louis Aragon's *Paysan de Paris*, which she has been unable to finish, the variations on the word Pessimism having thrown her off. All her remarks indicate a great revolutionary faith. Upon my request, she gives me her poem which I had found in the book and a few others as well, all of which are interesting. Her name is Fanny Beznos.

I also remember the apparently jocular proposition once made in my presence to a lady, asking that she present to the "Centrale Surréaliste" one of the remarkable sky-blue gloves she was carrying on a visit to us at this "Centrale," my sudden fear when I saw she was about to consent, and my supplications that she do nothing of the kind. I don't know what there can have been, at that moment, so terribly, so marvelously decisive for me in the thought of that glove leaving that hand forever. And even then this matter did not assume its true proportions, I mean those which it has retained, until after the moment this lady proposed coming back to lay on the table, on the very spot where I had so hoped she would not leave the blue glove, a bronze one she happened to possess and which I have subsequently seen at her home—also a woman's glove, the wrist folded over, the fingers flat—a glove I can never resist picking up, always astonished at its weight and interested, apparently, only in calculating its precise weight against what the other glove would not have weighed at all.

Only a few days ago, Louis Aragon pointed out to me that the sign of a Pourville hotel showing in red letters the words: MAISON ROUGE consisted of certain letters arranged in such a way that when seen from a certain angle in the street, the word MAISON disappeared and ROUGE read POLICE. This optical illusion would have no importance if on the same day, one or two hours later, the lady

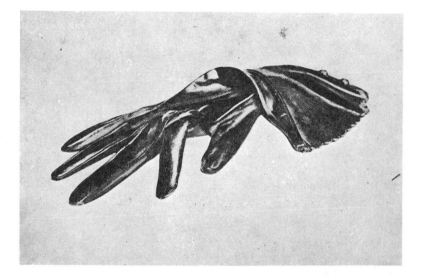

PLATE 16. Also a woman's glove . . .
(SEE PAGE 56)

PLATE 17. The *Humanité* bookstore

(SEE PAGE 63)

we shall call the *lady of the glove* had not taken me to see a *tableau changeant* which I had never heard of before and which was part of the furnishings in the house she had just rented. This object was an old engraving which, seen straight on, represents a tiger, but which, regarded perpendicularly to its surface of tiny vertical bands when you stand several feet to the left, represents a vase, and, from several feet to the right, an angel. I offer, in closing, these two facts because for me, under such conditions, their connection cannot be avoided and because I find it quite impossible to establish a rational correlation between them.

I hope, in any case, that the presentation of some dozen observations of this order as well as what follows will be of a nature to send some men rushing out into the street, after making them aware, if not of the non-existence, at least of the crucial inadequacy of any so-called categorical self-evaluation, of any action which requires a continuous application and which can be premeditated. The slightest occurrence, if it is truly unforeseen, turns all such things to idle talk. And after this, let no one speak to me of work—I mean the moral value of work. I am forced to accept the notion of work as a material necessity, and in this regard I strongly favor its better, that is its fairer, division. I admit that life's grim obligations make it a necessity, but never that I should believe in its value, revere my own or that of other men. I prefer, once again, walking by night to believing myself a man who walks by daylight. There is no use being alive if one must work. The event from which each of us is entitled to expect the revelation of his own life's meaning—that event which I may not yet have found, but on whose path I seek myself—*is not earned by work*. But I am anticipating, for perhaps it is this, more than anything else, that once made me understand and that now justifies, without further delay, Nadja's appearance on the scene.

Last of all, now, the tower of the Manoir d'Ango explodes and a snowfall of feathers from its doves dissolves on contact with the earth of the great courtyard once paved with scraps of tiles and now covered with real blood!

*L*ast October fourth, toward the end of one of those idle, gloomy afternoons I know so well how to spend, I happened to be in the Rue Lafayette: after stopping a few minutes at the stall outside the *Humanité* bookstore and buying Trotsky's latest work, I continued aimlessly in the direction of the Opéra. The offices and workshops were beginning to empty out from top to bottom of the buildings, doors were closing, people on the sidewalk were shaking hands, and already there were more people in the street now. I unconsciously watched their faces, their clothes, their way of walking. No, it was not yet these who would be ready to create the Revolution. I had just crossed an intersection whose name I don't know, in front of a church. Suddenly, perhaps still ten feet away, I saw a young, poorly dressed woman walking toward me, she had noticed me too, or perhaps had been watching me for several moments. She carried her head high, unlike everyone else on the sidewalk. And she looked so delicate she scarcely seemed to touch the ground as she walked. A faint smile may have been wandering across her face. She was curiously made up, as though beginning with her eyes, she had not had time to finish, though the rims of her eyes were dark for a blonde, the rims only, and not the lids (this effect is achieved, and achieved exclusively, by applying the mascara under the lid alone. It is interesting to note, in this regard, that Blanche Derval, as Solange, even when seen at close range, never seemed at all made up. Does this mean that what is only slightly permissible in the street but advisable in the theater is important to me only insofar as it has defied what is forbidden in one case, decreed in the other? Perhaps.) I had never seen such eyes. Without a moment's hesitation, I spoke to this unknown woman, though I must admit that I expected the worst. She smiled, but quite mysteriously and somehow *know-*

ingly, though I had no reason to think so. She was on her way, she claimed, to a hairdresser on the Boulevard Magenta (I say claimed because she later admitted she was going nowhere). She mentioned the financial difficulties she was having, even insisted on them, but apparently as a way of explaining the wretchedness of her appearance. We stopped at the terrace of a café near the Gare du Nord. I took a better look at her. What was so extraordinary about what was happening in those eyes? What was it they reflected—some obscure distress and at the same time some luminous pride? And also the riddle set by the beginning of a confession which, without asking me anything further, with a confidence which could (or which could not?) be misplaced, she made me. In Lille, her native city which she had left only two or three years ago, she had known a student she may have loved and who loved her. One fine day she decided to leave him when he least expected it, and this "for fear of getting in his way." This is when she came to Paris, writing him at increasingly longer intervals without ever giving her address. Nearly a year later, however, she ran into him in Paris itself and both of them were extremely surprised. Even as he took her hands, he could not help telling her how changed he found her, and then, still holding these hands, he was surprised to see how well manicured they were (though they are not at all so now). Then she too had mechanically looked at one of the hands holding hers and had not been able to restrain an exclamation upon noticing that the last two fingers were joined together. "But you've hurt yourself!" The young man was obliged to show her his other hand, which revealed the same deformity. She questions me about this for some time and with great feeling: "Is such a thing possible? To live so long with someone, to have every possible chance to observe him, to enjoy discovering his slightest physical and other peculiarities, and to end by knowing him so badly that you haven't ever noticed *that?* You think: you think love can do such things? And he was so angry, naturally, the only thing I could do was stop talking, those hands. . . . Then he said something I don't understand, there was a word in it I don't understand, he said: 'Ninny! I'm going back to Alsace-Lorraine. At least the women there know how to love.' Why: ninny? Do you know?" Naturally I react quite strongly to the sentence she has just quoted: "It doesn't matter. But I think generalizations about Alsace-Lorraine are vile, certainly the man was a fool, etc. . . . and then he left, you haven't seen him since? I'm glad to hear it." She told me her name, the one she had chosen for herself: "Nadja, because in Russian it's the beginning of the word hope, and because it's only the beginning." Just then she thinks of asking who I am (in the most limited sense of these words). I tell her. Then she returns to her past, speaks of her father, her mother. She is particularly moved by the memory of the former: "He was so weak! If you knew how weak he always was. When he was young, you see, no one ever refused him anything. His parents had always been so indulgent. There weren't automobiles then, but all the same a fine carriage, the coachman. . . . But for him everything melted away, and so quickly. . . . I love him so much. Each time I think of him, I tell myself how weak he is. . . . Oh, mother wasn't the same at all. She was a good woman, that's all, what everyone means by a *good* woman. Not the kind of wife my father needed at all. At home, of course, everything was always extremely clean, but you see, he wasn't the kind of man who could come home and find her in an apron. It's true he found a table set, or at least one there was plenty of time to set, but he didn't find what you call (with an ironic expression of greed and a funny gesture) a table *laid*. I love mother, you know, I wouldn't hurt her for anything in the world. So when I came to Paris, she knew I had a letter of reference to the Soeurs de Vaugirard. Of course I've never used it. But whenever I write her, I end my letter with these words: 'I hope I see you soon,' and I add: 'if God is willing, as Sister someone says,' and I put in any name that comes into my head.

And how happy that must make her! In the letters I get from her, what touches me most, what I'd give all the rest for, is the postscript. She always feels she should add: 'I wonder what you can be doing in Paris.' Poor mother, if she knew!" What Nadja is doing in Paris—but she wonders herself. Yes, evenings, around seven, she likes to be in the Metro, second-class. Most of the people in the car with her have finished their day's work. She sits down among them, and tries to detect from their expressions what they are thinking about. Naturally they are thinking about what they have left behind until tomorrow, only until tomorrow, and also of what is waiting for them this evening, which either relaxes or else makes them still more anxious. Nadja stares at something in the air: "They are good people." More moved than I care to show, this time I grow angry: "Oh no. Besides, that's not the point. People cannot be interesting insofar as they endure their work, with or without all their other troubles. How can that raise them up if the spirit of revolt is not uppermost within them? Besides, at such moments you see them and they don't see you. How I loathe the servitude people try to hold up to me as being so valuable. I pity the man who is condemned to it, who cannot generally escape it, but it is not the burden of his labor that disposes me in his favor, it is—it can only be—the vigor of his protest against it. I know that

at a factory furnace, or in front of one of those inex-
orable machines which all day long, at a few seconds'
interval, impose the repetition of the same gesture,
or anywhere else, under the least acceptable orders,
in a cell or before a firing squad, one can still feel
free: but it is not the martyrdom one undergoes
which creates this freedom. It is, I mean, a perpetual
unfettering: yet for this unfettering to be possible,
constantly possible, the fetters must not crush us,
as they do many of those you mention. But it is also,
and perhaps, in human terms, much more, the rela-
tively long but marvelous series of steps which man
may make unfettered. Do you suppose these people
capable of taking such steps? Have they even the
time for them? Have they the heart? Good people,
you said, yes, good people like those who get themselves killed in wars, isn't that what you mean?
Enough talk of heroes: a lot of unhappy men and a
few poor imbeciles. For myself, I admit such *steps*
are everything. Where do they lead, that is the
real question. Ultimately they all indicate a road,
and on this road, who knows if we will not find the
means of unfettering or of helping those unable to
follow it to unfetter themselves? It is only then that
we may loiter a little, though without turning back."
(What I can say on this subject is sufficiently apparent, particularly if I should ever decide to deal
with it concretely.) Nadja listened to me and made

no attempt to contradict my statements. Perhaps she had intended nothing less than an apology for labor. She begins telling me about her health, which is extremely delicate. The doctor she has consulted and whom she had picked out as a man she could trust, has, at the cost of all the money she had left, ordered her to leave for the Mont-Dore at once. This notion delights her, since such a trip is so unfeasible for her. But she has convinced herself that some arduous form of manual labor might somehow substitute for the cure she cannot take. Therefore she attempted to get a job in a bakery, and even in a pork-butcher's, where, as she decided in her purely poetic way, there are more reasons to feel well than elsewhere. Everyone offered her ridiculously low salaries. It also turned out that before she even received an answer she was closely scrutinized. One master baker, who promised her seventeen francs a day, after having glanced at her a second time corrected himself: "seventeen or eighteen." And she, playfully: "I told him: for seventeen, yes; for eighteen, no." Now we are walking through the narrow Rue du Faubourg-Poissonière, I think. It is dinnertime. I want to say goodbye. She asks who is expecting me. "My wife." "Married! Oh, well then . . ." and in a voice suddenly very serious, very composed: "that's too bad. But . . . and this great idea of yours? I was just beginning to understand it so well. It was really a star, a star you were heading toward. You can't fail to reach it. Hearing you speak, I felt that nothing would hold you back, nothing, not even me. . . . You could never see this star as I do. You don't understand: It's like the heart of a heartless flower." I am deeply moved. To distract her, I ask Nadja where she is having dinner. And suddenly that frivolity which is hers alone, perhaps, to put it precisely, that freedom, flashes out: "Where?" (pointing): "oh, over there, or there˙(the two nearest restaurants), wherever I happen to be, you know. It's always this way." About to leave her, I want to ask one question which sums up all the rest, a question which only I would ever ask, probably, but which has at least once found a reply worthy of it: "Who are you?" And she, without a moment's hesitation: "I am the soul in limbo." We separate, agreeing to meet the next day at the bar at the corner of the Rue Lafayette and the Rue du Faubourg Poissonière. She makes me promise to bring her some of my books, though I urge her not to read them. Life is other than what one writes. She keeps me a few minutes more to tell me what it is about me that touches her. It is—in the way I think, speak, in my whole manner, apparently: and this is one of the compliments which has moved me most in my whole life— my *simplicity*.

October 5.—Nadja is here first, ahead of time. She no longer looks the way she did yesterday. Rather elegant today, in black and red, with an extremely pretty hat which she takes off, revealing her straw-colored hair which has lost its incredible disorder, silk stockings and shoes which, unlike yesterday's, are quite presentable. The conversation has also become more difficult and starts on her part with a number of hesitations. This lasts until she seizes the books I have brought (*Les Pas Perdus, Manifeste du Surréalisme*): "Lost steps? But there's no such thing!" She leafs through the book with great curiosity. Her eye is caught by one of Jarry's poems quoted in the book:

Parmi les bruyères, penil des menhirs . . .

Far from discouraging her, this poem, which she first reads through quite quickly and then examines in detail, seems to move her deeply. At the end of the second quatrain, her eyes brim and are filled with the vision of a forest. She sees the poet passing near this wood, as though she could follow him at a distance: "No, he's skirting the forest. He cannot enter, he does not enter." Then she loses him and returns to the poem at a point just before the place where she left it, asking about the words that surprise her most, according each the precise sign of intelligence, of assent it requires.

Chasse de leur acier la martre et l'hermine.

"With their steel? The marten . . . and the ermine. Yes, I see; the freezing burrows, the cold rivers: *De leur acier*." A little further on:

En mangeant le bruit des hannetons, C'havann

(Frightened, closing the book): "Oh! That must be death!"

The contrast in color between the covers of the two volumes surprises and pleases her. Apparently it "suits" me. I must have chosen them on purpose (which I did). Then she tells me about two friends she has had: one, when she first came to Paris, whom she habitually refers to as "Dear friend," that was the way she used to address him and he always insisted she remain ignorant of who he was; she still indicates great veneration for him, a man close to seventy-five, who lived in the colonies a long time, and who told her when he left that he was returning to Senegal. The other is an American, who seems to have inspired her with feelings of quite another order: "Besides, he called me Lena, in memory of his daughter who had died. That was very affectionate, very touching of him, wasn't it? But you know, I found I couldn't stand being called that, as if it was a dream: Lena, Lena. . . . So I would move my hand in front of his eyes several times, quite close to his eyes, like this, and I would say: 'No, not Lena, Nadja.'" We leave the bar. She continues: "I see your house. Your wife. She is dark, of course. Short. Pretty. Now I see a dog beside her. Perhaps a cat too, but somewhere else (this is correct). Now I don't see anything else." I am about to go home, Nadja joins me in the taxi. We remain silent for a while, then she suddenly addresses me using *tu:* "A game: say something. Close your eyes and say something. Anything, a number, a name. Like this (she closes her eyes): Two, two what? Two women. What do they look like? Wearing black. Where are they? In a park. . . . And then, what are they doing? Try it, it's so easy, why don't you want to play? You know, that's how I talk to myself when I'm alone, I tell myself all kinds of stories. And not only silly stories: actually, I live this way altogether." * I leave her at my door: "And what about me now? Where shall I go? But it's so easy to return slowly toward the Rue Lafayette, the Rue du Faubourg Poissonière—to begin by going back to the very spot where we were."

October 6.—So as not to have too far to walk, I go out about four intending to stop in at the "Nouvelle France," where Nadja is supposed to meet me

---

* Does this not approach the extreme limit of the surrealist aspiration, its *furthest determinant?*

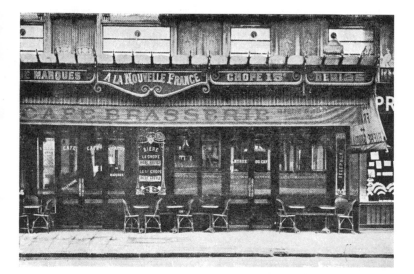

PLATE 18. At the "Nouvelle France"

(SEE PAGE 74)

at five-thirty. This gives me time to take a stroll around the boulevards: not far from the Opéra, I have to pick up my pen at a shop where it is being repaired. For a change I decide to take the right sidewalk of the Rue de la Chausée-d'Antin. One of the first people I prepare to meet there is Nadja, looking as she did the first day I saw her. She advances as if she didn't want to see me. She seems quite unable to explain her presence here in this street where, to forestall further questions, she tells me she is looking for Dutch chocolate. Without even thinking about it, we have already turned around and go into the first café we come to. Nadja keeps a certain distance between us, she even seems rather suspicious. For instance, she looks into my hat, probably to read the initials on the band, though she pretends to be doing it quite unconsciously, it being her habit to determine certain men's nationality without their knowing it. She admits she had intended to miss the rendezvous we had agreed upon. I noticed when we met today that she was holding the copy of *Les Pas Perdus* I had lent her. Now it is on the table and, giving it a side-long glance, I remark that only a few pages are cut: those of the article called "L'esprit nouveau," in which is actually described a striking series of en-counters that Louis Aragon, André Derain, and my-self had one day a few minutes apart. The indecision each of us betrayed under the circumstances; our common difficulty in characterizing what we had just experienced; the curious mystical appeal which obliged Aragon and me to return to the very places where this veritable sphinx had appeared to us in the guise of a charming woman crossing from one sidewalk to the other to question the by-passers (this sphinx who had spared us, one after the other) obliging us, in our search for her, to run along any axis which might connect, however whimsically, these places; the lack of results of this pursuit which the time that had elapsed would have made hopeless— this is what Nadja immediately turned to. She is astonished and disappointed by the fact that I had considered commentaries on the account of the day's brief occurrences quite superfluous. She urges me to explain what I believe the article means as it stands, and, since I have published it, the degree of objectivity I attribute to it. I am obliged to reply that I know nothing about it, that in such matters the right to bear witness seems to me to be all that is granted, that I have been the first victim of this abuse of confidence, if that is what it is, but I can see that she is not going to let me off, I read first impatience, then consternation in her eyes. Perhaps she imagines I am lying: a certain embarrassment persists between us. When she mentions going home, I offer to accompany her. She gives the driver the address of the Théâtre des Arts which, she tells me, is only a few steps from the building where she lives. On the way, she stares at me in silence for a long time. Then her eyes close and open again quite rapidly, as when you are with someone you have not seen for a long time or did not expect to see again, and as if to signify that you "don't believe them." She seems to be suffering from a certain inner conflict, but suddenly she surrenders, closes her eyes for good, offers me her lips. . . . Now she tells me of my power over her, of my faculty for making her think and do whatever I desire, perhaps more than I think I desire. Because of this, she begs me to do nothing against her. She feels she has never had any secrets from me, long before knowing me. A brief scene in dialogue at the end of my "Poisson Soluble," and which seems to be all she has yet read of the *Manifeste*, a scene whose precise meaning moreover, I have never been able to determine and whose characters are as alien, their agitation as enigmatic as possible—as if they had been tendered and swept away again by a flood of sand—gives her the impression of having actually participated in it and even of having played the—if anything obscure—part of Hélène.* The place, the at-

* I have never known personally any woman of this name, which has always irritated me, just as that of Solange has always delighted me. Yet Madame Sacco, clairvoyante, 3 Rue des Usines, who has never been mistaken about me, assured me early this year that my mind was greatly occupied with a "Hélène." Is this why, some time after this

mosphere, the respective attitudes of the speakers were indeed what I had imagined. She wants to show me "where this happened": I propose we dine together. There must be a certain confusion in her mind, for she has us driven not to the Ile Saint-Louis, as she supposes, but to the Place Dauphine, where, curiously enough, another episode of "Poisson Soluble" occurs: "A kiss is so quickly forgotten." (The Place Dauphine is certainly one of the most profoundly secluded places I know of, one of the worst wastelands in Paris. Whenever I happen to be there, I feel the desire to go somewhere else gradually ebbing out of me, I have to struggle against myself to get free from a gentle, over-insistent, and, finally, crushing embrace. Besides, I lived for some time in a hotel near this square, the City Hotel, where the comings and goings at all hours, for anyone not satisfied with oversimplified solutions, are suspect.) The light is fading. In order to be alone, we have our dinner served outside by the wine seller. For the first time, during the meal, Nadja behaves rather frivolously. A drunkard keeps prowling around our table. He shouts some incoherent words in a pro-

---

period, I was so greatly interested in everything concerning *Hélène Smith?* The conclusion is evidently on the order of that previously imposed upon me by the fusion in a dream of two extremely disparate images. "Hélène, c'est moi," Nadja used to say.

PLATE 19. Madame Sacco, clairvoyante,
3 Rue des Usines
(SEE PAGE 79)

PLATE 20. We have our dinner
served outside by the wine seller
(SEE PAGE 80)

testing tone. Among them continually recur one or two obscene words which he emphasizes. His wife, watching him from under the trees, confines herself to shouting at him occasionally: "All right, are you coming?" I try to get rid of him several times, but without success. When the dessert is served, Nadja begins looking around her. She is certain that an underground tunnel passes under our feet, starting at the Palais de Justice (she shows me which part of the building, slightly to the right of the white flight of steps) and circling the Hôtel Henri IV. She is disturbed by the thought of what has already occurred in this square and will occur here in the future. Where only two or three couples are at this moment fading into the darkness, she seems to see a crowd. "And the dead, the dead!" The drunkard lugubriously continues cracking jokes. Nadja's eyes now sweep over the surrounding houses. "Do you see that window up there? It's black, like all the rest. Look hard. In a minute it will light up. It will be red." The minute passes. The window lights up. There are, as a matter of fact, red curtains. (I am sorry, but I am unable to do anything about the fact that this may exceed the limits of credibility. Nevertheless, in dealing with such a subject, I should never forgive myself for taking sides: I confine myself to *granting* that this window, being black, has now become red, and that is all.) I confess that this place frightens me, as it is beginning to frighten Nadja too. "How terrible! Can you see what's going on in the trees? The blue and the wind, the blue wind. I've seen that blue wind pass through these same trees only once before. It was there, from a window in the Hôtel Henri IV,* and my friend, the second man I told you about, was about to leave. And there was a voice saying: 'You're going to die, you're going to die.' I didn't want to die, but I felt so dizzy. . . . I'd certainly have fallen if he hadn't held me back." I decide it is high time we leave. As we walk along the quais, I feel that Nadja is trembling all over. She is the one who wanted to walk back toward the Conciergerie. She is very abandoned in her behavior, very sure of me. But she is looking for something, she insists that we walk into a courtyard, a courtyard of some police station, which she rapidly explores. "It's not here. . . . Listen, tell me why you have to go to prison? What is it you're going to do? I've been to prison too. Who was I? It was ages ago. And you, then, who were you?" Now we are walking along the iron railing again, when suddenly Nadja refuses to go any further. Here on the right, is a low window that overlooks the moat, and she cannot take her eyes off it. It is in front of this window which

* Which faces the house just discussed: this too for the partisans of easy solutions.

looks so forlorn that we must wait, she knows that much. It is from here that everything can come. It is here that everything begins. She holds on to the railing with both hands so that I will not pull her away. She virtually stops answering my questions. For the sake of peace I wait until she is ready to continue of her own free will. She has not forgotten about the underground tunnel and probably imagines she is at one of its exits. She wonders who she might have been, in Marie-Antoinette's circle. The footsteps of passers-by make her shudder for a long time. I am concerned, and lifting her hands from the fence one after the other, I manage to make her follow me. More than a half hour goes by this way. Once we cross the bridge, we head toward the Louvre. Nadja is still upset. To restore her, I recite a poem by Baudelaire but the inflections of my voice terrify her all over again, her fear aggravated by her memory of the kiss we exchanged a little while before, "a kiss with a threat in it." She stops again, leans on the stone wall, her eyes and mine gazing into the river that is now sparkling with lights: "That hand, that hand on the Seine, why is that hand flaming over the water? It's true that fire and water are the same thing. But what does that hand mean? How do you interpret it? Let me look at that hand! Why do you want to go away now? What are you afraid of?

You think I'm very sick, don't you? I'm not sick.
But what do you think that means: fire and water,
a hand of fire over the water? (Joking): Of course
it's not good luck: fire and water are the same thing,
fire and gold are quite different." Toward midnight
we reach the Tuileries, where she wants to sit down
for a moment. We are in front of a fountain, whose
jet she seems to be watching. "Those are your
thoughts and mine. Look where they all start from,
how high they reach, and then how it's still prettier
when they fall back. And then they dissolve immediately, driven back up with the same strength, then
there's that broken spurt again, that fall . . . and
so on indefinitely." I exclaim: "But Nadja, how
strange! Where did you get such an image—it's expressed in almost the same form in a work you can't
have seen and which I've just finished reading?"
(And I am obliged to explain that this image is the
object of a vignette preceding the third of Berkeley's
Dialogues between Hylas and Philonous, in the 1750
edition, where it is accompanied by the legend:
"*Urget aquas vis sursum eadem, flectit que deorsum,*"
which at the end of the book, from the point of
view of the defense of the idealist attitude, becomes
of essential significance.) But she does not listen to
me, her attention is monopolized by the behavior of
a man passing back and forth in front of us whom
she thinks she knows, for this is not the first time

PLATE 21. We are in front of a fountain,
whose jet she seems to be watching
(SEE PAGE 86)

Urget aquas vis sursum eadem flectit quæ deorsum.

TROISIÉME

DIALOGUE

 HILONOÜS. Hé bien, *Hyla*
quels font les fruits de vos m
ditations d'hier? vous ont e

PLATE 22. Preceding the third of the
Dialogues between Hylas and Philonous . . .
(SEE PAGE 86)

that she has been in these gardens at such an hour.
This man, if he is the one, once asked her to marry
him. This reminds her of her little daughter, a child
of whose existence she has informed me with so many
precautions and whom she adores, particularly because she resembles other children so little, "with
their mania for taking out their dolls' eyes to see
what's there behind them." Nadja knows that she
always attracts children: wherever she is, they tend
to cluster around her, to come and smile at her. Now
she is talking as though to herself, her head is turned
away from me, I begin to feel tired. But without my
having shown the slightest sign of impatience: "One
thing, that's all. I suddenly felt I was going to hurt
you. (Turning round to face me): It's over." We
leave the garden and lose no time getting to another
bar, in the Rue Saint-Honoré, which is called Le
Dauphin. Nadja remarks that we have come from
the Place Dauphine to the Dauphin. (In that game
which consists of finding a resemblance with some
animal, people usually agree that I am a dolphin.)
Nadja cannot endure the sight of a mosaic strip ex-
tending from the counter across the floor, and we
must leave the bar only a moment after we have
come in. She has our driver stop in front of the
Théâtre des Arts. We agree to meet again at the
"Nouvelle France," but not until the evening of the
day after tomorrow.

October 7.—I have suffered from a violent head-
ache which, perhaps mistakenly, I attribute to last
night's emotions and also to the effort of attention,
of accommodation which I have had to make. The
whole morning, too, I have been bothering myself
about Nadja; it was a mistake not having made a
date with her today. I am annoyed. I suppose I observe her too much, but how can I help it? How
does she regard me, how does she judge me? It is
unforgivable of me to go on seeing her if I do not
love her. Don't I love her? When I am near her I
am nearer things which are near her. In her condi-
tion, she is certainly going to need me, one way or
another, and suddenly. It would be hateful to refuse
whatever she asks of me, one way or another, for
she is so pure, so free of any earthly tie, and cares
so little, but so marvelously, for life. She was trembling yesterday, perhaps from cold: so lightly dressed.
It would also be unforgivable if I were not to reassure her about the kind of interest I feel in her
behalf, persuade her that she could not be an object
of mere curiosity for me—how could she think so—
a whim. What should I do? And to have to wait
until tomorrow night—no, that is impossible. What
can I do in the meantime, if I don't see her? And if
I never see her again? I wouldn't *know* any more.
And I should therefore have deserved not to know
any more. And it would never happen again. There

might be some of those false annunciations, those pro-
visional moments of grace, real death-traps of the
soul, an abyss, an abyss into which the splendidly
mournful bird of divination has vanished again. What
can I do, around six, except go to the bar where we
have already met? No chance of finding her there,
of course, unless. . . . But "unless"—is it not here
that the great possibility of Nadja's intervention
resides, quite beyond any question of luck? I go out
at three with my wife and a friend; in the taxi we
continue discussing Nadja, as we have been doing
during lunch. Suddenly, while I am paying no attention whatever to the people on the street, some
sudden vividness on the left-hand sidewalk, at the
corner of Saint-Georges, makes me almost mechanically knock on the window. It is as if Nadja had
just passed by. I run, completely at random, in one
of the three directions she might have taken. And
as a matter of fact it is Nadja, she has stopped now,
talking to a man who, it seems to me was accom-
panying her a moment before. She leaves him quite
suddenly to join me. In the café, the conversation
begins awkwardly. This is the second consecutive
day I have met her: it is apparent that she is at my
mercy. If this is the case, she is behaving with extreme
reticence. Her material circumstances are quite desperate, since in order to be able to improve them,
it would be better for her not to know me. She

makes me touch her dress to show me how sturdy
it is, "but at the expense of every other quality."
She can no longer run up debts and she is resisting
the threats of her landlord and his dreadful sugges-
tions. She makes no secret of the means she would
employ to obtain money for herself if I did not exist,
though she no longer has even the sum necessary to
have her hair done and to go afterwards to the
Claridge, where, inevitably. . . . "I can't help it,"
she says, laughing, "money gets away from me. Besides, everything is over now. Once—only once—I
happened to have twenty-five thousand francs, which
my friend had left me. He assured me that in a few
days I could easily *triple* this amount if I went to
the Hague and bought cocaine with it. I was given
thirty-five thousand francs more for the same purpose. The mission was accomplished very easily: two
days later I was bringing two kilos of the drug in
my bag. The trip was made under the best conditions. Yet as I got off the train, I heard something
like a voice saying: 'you won't get by.' I was barely
on the platform when a man, a perfect stranger, came
up to me. 'Excuse me' he said, 'But do I have the
honor of speaking to Mademoiselle D . . . ?'—'Yes,
but please, I don't know. . . .'—'That doesn't matter
in the least, Mademoiselle. Here is my card,' and
he takes me to the police station. There I am asked
what I have in my bag. Naturally I tell them, open-

ing it to show them. So. I was released the same day, thanks to the intervention of a friend of mine, a lawyer or a judge named G. . . . I wasn't even interrogated further, and I was so upset I even forgot to say that all the cocaine wasn't in my bag and they would have to look for it under my hatband too. But the amount they would have to look for there wasn't worth the bother. I kept it for myself. I swear that's all been over and done with a long time." Now she is unfolding a letter she wants to show me. It is from a man she met one Sunday at the stage door of the Théâtre-Français. He must be an employee, since it has taken him several days to write her and since *he did so only at the beginning of the month.* She could telephone now, to him or to someone else, but she cannot bring herself to do so. It is all too obvious that money gets away from her. I ask her how much she needs right away: five hundred francs. Not having this sum with me, I offer to give it to her the next day. All her anxiety has disappeared. Once again I enjoy that delightful mixture of frivolity and fervor. Respectfully I kiss her lovely teeth and she says, slowly, gravely, the second time a few notes higher than the first: "Communion takes place in silence. . . . Communion takes place in silence." This, she explains, is because this kiss leaves her with the impression of something sacred, where her teeth "substituted for the host."

October 8.—When I wake up I open Aragon's letter from Italy; with it is a photographic reproduction of the central detail of a painting by Ucello unfamiliar to me. This painting is called: *The Profanation of the Host.** Toward the end of the day, which passes without other incidents, I go to the customary bar (the "Nouvelle France") where I wait for Nadja in vain. More than ever, I fear that she has disappeared. My only recourse is to try and find out where she lives, somewhere near the Théâtre des Arts. I manage this without difficulty: she is registered in the third hotel I inquire at, the Hôtel du Théâtre, Rue de Cheroy. Not finding her in, I leave a letter in which I ask how to get her the money she needed so badly the day before yesterday.

October 9.—Nadja telephoned me at home while I was out. To the person who answered the telephone and asked her how I could reach her, she replied: "I cannot be reached." But a little later, she invites me by *pneumatique* to stop by the bar at five-thirty. I find her there, in fact. Her absence of the day before was the result of a misunderstanding: this once we had made our appointment at the Régence, and

---

* I saw it reproduced in its entirety only several months later. It seemed to me full of hidden intentions and, in all respects, quite difficult to interpret.

PLATE 23. *The Profanation of the Host*
(SEE PAGE 94)

PLATE 24. I had recently become
greatly interested in this period . . .

it is I who forgot it. I give her the money.* She cries. We are alone in the bar when in comes a kind of peddler I have never seen before. He offers a few crudely colored prints for sale, mostly French historical scenes. The one he shows me, which he insists I take from him, represents the most striking episodes of the reigns of Louis VI and Louis VII (I had recently become greatly interested in this period, since it is that of the "Courts of Love," imagining with great intensity what life might have been like during that period). The old man provides extremely confused commentaries for each of the illustrations and I cannot make out what he is saying about Suger. For the price of two francs, which I give him, as well as two more to make him go away, he absolutely insists on giving us all his pictures as well as about ten glossy color postcards of women. It is impossible to dissuade him from doing this. He leaves walking backwards: "God bless you, sir." Now Nadja makes me read the letters which have recently been sent to her. These letters are of little interest to me. Some are tearful, some declamatory, some absurd—all signed by G . . . , whom I have already mentioned. However, G . . . is the name of that President of the Assize Court who, during Madame Sierri's trial for murder some days before, had

* Three times the agreed amount, which, as I have only just realized, is certainly a coincidence.

permitted himself an atrocious remark, telling the accused woman that to have killed her lover she did not even have "the gratitude of her own womb (*laughter*)." And as a matter of fact, Paul Eluard had asked someone to look up this name which, since he had forgotten it, had remained blank in the manuscript of the "Revue de la presse" intended for *La Révolution Surréaliste*. I notice with uneasiness that a pair of scales is printed on the back of the envelopes I am looking at.

October 10.—We are having dinner on the Quai Malaquais, in the Restaurant Delaborde. The waiter is extremely clumsy. He seems to be fascinated by Nadja. He fusses needlessly around our table, brushing imaginary crumbs from the cloth, moving her bag, apparently quite incapable of remembering our orders. Nadja laughs up her sleeve and tells me that there is more to come. And as a matter of fact, though he serves the nearby tables without incident, he spills wine around our glasses and, taking infinite precautions to put one plate down in its place, jostles another which falls to the floor and breaks. From the beginning of the meal to the end (this too is almost unbelievable) eleven plates are broken. Each time this waiter comes into the room from the kitchen, he is facing our table, and the minute he glances up he seems to have a dizzy spell. This is both funny and painful. Finally he no longer dares approach our table, and we have considerable difficulty finishing our dinner. Nadja is not at all surprised. She knows her power over certain men, for example over Negroes who, wherever she may be, are compelled to come and talk to her. She tells me that at three o'clock, at the ticket window of the Le Peletier Métro station, she was given a new ten-franc piece which she held tight between her hands all the way down the stairs. To the man punching the tickets she said: "Heads or tails?" He answered tails. Tails it was. "You were wondering, Mademoiselle, if you would be seeing your friend just now. You'll see him." We walk along the quays toward the Institut de France. She speaks to me again of the man she refers to as "Dear friend," and to whom she says she owes whatever she is. "Without him, I would be the worst wretch you can imagine." I discover that he put her to sleep every night, after dinner. She took several months to realize this. He made her tell him about her day down to the last detail, approved what he considered good, criticized the rest. And always, afterwards, a physical pain localized in her head kept her from repeating what he must have forbidden her. This man, lost in his white beard, who wanted her to be totally ignorant about himself, impressed her as a king. Everywhere she went with him, she felt there was an extremely respectful

movement of attention as he passed. Yet, afterwards
she saw him again one evening, on the bench of a
Métro station, and she thought he looked exhausted,
very bedraggled, and greatly aged. We reach the
corner of the Rue de Seine, where we turn, Nadja
no longer wishing to continue straight ahead. She is
still quite distressed, and tells me to follow a line
slowly traced across the sky by a hand. "Still that
hand." She shows it to me, as a matter of fact, on
a poster, a little beyond the Dorbon bookstore. It
so happens that there is, high above us, a red hand
with its index finger pointing, advertising something
or other. Nadja insists on touching this hand, which
she jumps up to reach several times and which she
succeeds in slapping with her own. "The hand of
fire, it's all you, you know, it's you." She falls silent
for a while, I suspect she has tears in her eyes. Then
suddenly, standing in front of me, virtually stopping
me, with that extraordinary way she has of calling
me, the way you might call someone from room to
room in an empty castle: "André? André? . . . You
will write a novel about me. I'm sure you will. Don't
say you won't. Be careful: everything fades, everything vanishes. Something must remain of us. . . .
But it doesn't matter: you'll take another name: and
the name you choose, I ought to tell you, is extremely
important. It must have something of fire about it,
for it is always fire that recurs in anything to do

with you. The hand too, but that is less essential
than the fire. What I see is a flame starting from the
wrist, like this (with the gesture of palming a card),
and making the hand burn up immediately, so that
it disappears in the twinkling of an eye. You'll find
a Latin or Arabic pseudonym.* Promise. You have
to." She uses a new image to make me understand
how she lives: it's like the morning when she bathes
and her body withdraws while she stares at the surface of the bath water. "I am the thought on the
bath in the room without mirrors." She had forgotten
to tell me about the strange adventure which happened to her last night, toward eight o'clock, when,
supposing herself alone, she was singing and dancing
as she walked beneath an arcade of the Palais Royal.
An old woman appeared before a closed door and
Nadja supposed she was going to ask her for money.
But the old woman was merely in need of a pencil.
Nadja lent her hers and the old woman went through
the motions of scribbling some words on a visiting
card before slipping it under the door. Then she gave
Nadja a similar card, explaining that she had come
to see Madame Camée and that the latter was unfortunately not in. This scene took place in front of
a shop over whose door could be read the words:

* On the doors of many Arab houses is drawn, it seems,
the emblematic outline of a red hand: this is the hand
of Fatima.

CAMÉES DURS. This old woman looked a great deal like a witch. I examine the tiny card Nadja insists on leaving with me: "Madame Aubry-Abrivard, woman of letters, 20 Rue de Varenne, fourth floor, right." This story seems to require an explanation. Nadja, who has thrown a fold of her cape back over her shoulder, assumes with an astonishing facility the arrogance of the Devil as he appears in romantic prints. It is very dark and very cold. As I come close to her, I am startled to notice that she is literally "trembling like a leaf."

October 11.—Paul Eluard went to the address given on the card. He found no one there. On the door indicated was pinned, but upside down, an envelope with these words: "Today, October 11, Madame Aubry-Abrivard will be home very late, but will certainly return." I am in an extremely bad mood after a conversation I have had this afternoon and which has been pointlessly extended. Besides, Nadja has come late and I expect nothing extraordinary from her. We wander through the streets together, but quite separately. She repeats several times this sentence whose syllables she emphasizes more and more heavily: "Time is a tease. Time is a tease—because everything has to happen in its own time." It is exasperating to see her reading the menus outside restaurants and punning with the names of

PLATE 25. CAMÉES DURS

(SEE PAGE 102)

PLATE 26. The Sphinx-Hôtel, Boulevard Magenta
(SEE PAGE 105)

certain dishes. I am bored. We pass the Sphinx-Hôtel, Boulevard Magenta. She shows me the luminous sign with the words that made her decide to stay here the night she arrived in Paris. She remained several months, receiving no visits save those of the "Dear friend" who passed for her uncle.

October 12.—I have asked Max Ernst if he would paint Nadja's portrait. But Madame Sacco has predicted he will meet a woman named Nadia or Natasha whom he will not like and who will do physical harm to the woman he loves. This counter-indication seems sufficient to us. A little after four, in a café on the Boulevard des Batignolles, once again I must pretend to discover G . . .'s letters, filled with entreaties and accompanied by stupid poems plagiarized from Musset. Then Nadja lets me have a drawing, the first of hers I have seen, which she made the other day at La Régence while she was waiting for me. She is glad to explain the meaning of the principal elements of this drawing, except for the rectangular mask about which she can say nothing save that this is how it looks to her. The black cat in the middle of the forehead is the nail by which it is attached; along the dotted line we find first of all, a hook; the black star in the upper section represents the idea. But what, according to Nadja, constitutes the chief interest of this page, without my managing to learn why, is the calligraphy of the L's. After dinner, walking around the garden of the Palais Royal, her dream seems to have assumed a mythological character I had hitherto not discerned. With great skill, so that she gives the striking illusion of reality, she briefly evokes the elusive character of Melusina. Then she asks me point-blank: "Who killed the Gorgon, tell me, tell." I have more and more difficulty following her monologue, which long silences begin to make unintelligible. Rather late, I suggest that we leave Paris. For this purpose we go to the Gare Saint-Lazare where I buy tickets for Saint-Germain. The train is leaving as we approach the platform. We must wait over an hour for the eleven-thirty train. We walk up and down the waiting room. Suddenly, as on the previous day a drunkard begins prowling around us. He complains he cannot find where he is going and asks me to take him out to the street. Nadja is no longer withdrawn. As she points out, it is true that everyone—even people in a great hurry—is turning around to look at us; it isn't Nadja they're looking at, but *us*. "They can't believe it, you see, they can't get over seeing us together. That's how rare that fire is in your eyes, and in mine." We are alone now, in a first-class compartment. All her confidence, her attention, her hope have returned to me. Suppose we got off the train at Le Vésinet? She would like to walk a little in the woods. Why not? But suddenly, as I am kissing her, she screams. "There (pointing to the top of the window), someone's there. I just saw a head upside down—very clearly." I reassure her as well as I can. Five minutes later, the same thing happens: "I tell you he's there, he has a cap on! No, it's not a vision. I know when it's a vision." I lean out the window: nothing for the entire length of this car, nor on the steps of the next. Yet Nadja insists she couldn't have made a mistake. She stubbornly stares at the top of the window and remains quite upset. To set her mind at rest, I lean outside again. I have time to see, quite distinctly, the head of a man who is lying on the train roof disappear over our compartment, and as a matter of fact he is wearing a trainman's cap. Probably a railroad employee who can get up there from the outside of the adjacent second-class car without difficulty. At the next station, while Nadja stands at the window and I watch as the passengers get off the train, a man about to leave the station throws her a kiss. A second man does the same thing, then a third. She receives this kind of homage with both satisfaction and gratitude. It always happens to her, and she seems to enjoy it a great deal. At Le Vésinet, where everything is closed for the night, it is impossible to find lodgings. The prospect of wandering through the woods is no longer very alluring. We decide to wait for the next train to Saint-

Germain. We get on there, about one in the morning and go to the Hôtel du Prince de Galles. As we walk in front of the château, Nadja says she wants to be Madame de Chevreuse; how gracefully she conceals her face behind the heavy, nonexistent plume of her hat!

.   .   .   .

Can it be that this desperate pursuit comes to an end here? Pursuit of what I do not know, but pursuit, in order to set working all the artifices of intellectual seduction. Nothing—not the glitter, when they are cut, of rare metals such as sodium—nor the phosphorescence, in certain regions, of stone quarries—nor the splendid glow over mine-shafts—nor the crackling of wood of a clock I throw on the fire so it will die as it chimes the hours—nor the fascination which, despite everything, *The Embarcation for Cytherea* exerts upon me when I determine that despite the various postures and attitudes, it displays only one couple—nor the majesty of reservoir landscapes—nor the charm of naked walls with their flowered papers and their shadows of mantlepieces, in apartment houses under demolition: nothing of all this, nothing of what constitutes my own light for me has been forgotten. Who were we, confronting reality, that reality which I know now was

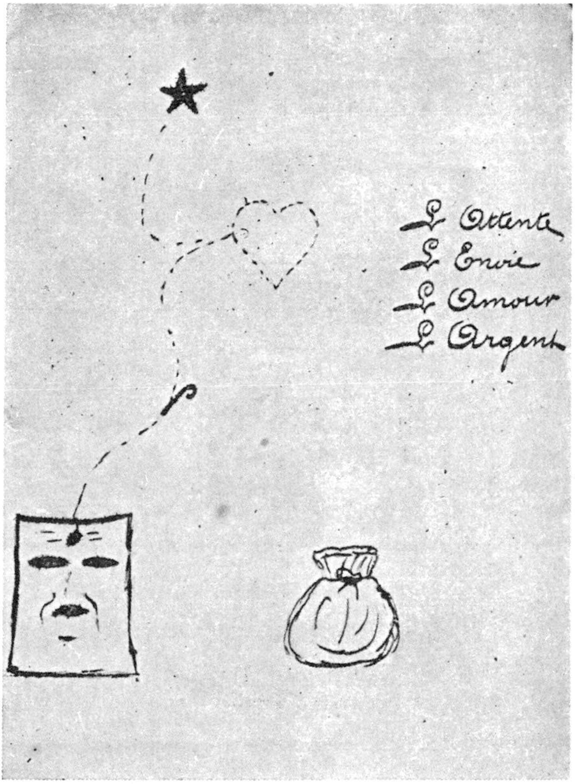

PLATE 27. Except for the rectangular mask
about which she can say nothing . . .
(SEE PAGE 105)

PLATE 28. Here, high in the château,
in the right-hand tower . . .
(SEE PAGE 112)

lying at Nadja's feet like a lapdog? By what latitude could we, abandoned thus to the fury of symbols, be occasionally a prey to the demon of analogy, seeing ourselves the object of extreme overtures, of singular, special attentions? How does it happen that thrown together, once and for all, so far from the earth, in those brief intervals which our marvelous stupor grants us, we have been able to exchange a few incredibly concordant views above the smoking debris of old ideas and sempiternal life? I have taken Nadja, from the first day to the last, for a free genius, something like one of those spirits of the air which certain magical practices momentarily permit us to entertain but which we can never overcome. As for her, I know that in every sense of the word, she takes me for a god, she thinks of me as the sun. I also remember—and at this moment there can be nothing both more beautiful and more tragic—I remember having appeared black and cold to her, like a man struck by lightning, lying at the feet of the Sphinx. I have seen her fern-colored eyes *open* mornings on a world where the beating of hope's great wings is scarcely distinct from the other sounds which are those of terror and, upon such a world, I had as yet seen eyes do nothing but close. I know that for Nadja this *departure* from a point so rare, so foolhardy to hope even to reach, was effected by scorning everything customarily invoked at the moment one drowns, voluntarily remote from the last raft, at the cost of everything that comprises the false but virtually irresistible compensations of life. Here, high in the château, in the right-hand tower, there is a room which, certainly, no one would dream of showing us, which we would perhaps be wrong to visit—there is scarcely reason to try—but which, according to Nadja, is all that we would need to know in Saint-Germain, in fact.* How much I admire those men who decide to be shut up at night in a museum in order to examine at their own discretion, at an illicit time, some portrait of a woman they illuminate by a dark lantern. Inevitably, afterwards, they must know much more about such a woman than we do. Perhaps life needs to be deciphered like a cryptogram. Secret staircases, frames from which the paintings quickly slip aside and vanish (giving way to an archangel bearing a sword or to those who must forever advance), buttons which must be indirectly pressed to make an entire room move sideways or vertically, or immediately change all its furnishings; we may imagine the mind's greatest adventure as a journey of this sort to the paradise of pitfalls. Who is the real Nadja

---

* It was Louis VI who, at the beginning of the twelfth century, built a royal castle in the Forest of Laye, the origin of the present château and of the town of Saint-Germain.

—the one who told me she had wandered all night long in the Forest of Fontainebleau with an archeologist who was looking for some stone remains which, certainly, there was plenty of time to find by daylight—but suppose it was this man's passion!—I mean, is the real Nadja this always inspired and inspiring creature who enjoyed being nowhere but in the streets, the only region of valid experience for her, in the street, accessible to interrogation from any human being launched upon some great chimera, or (why not admit it) the one who sometimes *fell*, since, after all, others had felt authorized to speak to her, had been able to see in her only the most wretched of women, and the least protected? Sometimes I reacted with terrible violence against the over-detailed account she gave me of certain scenes of her past life, concerning which I decided, probably quite superficially, that her dignity could not have survived entirely intact. A story of a blow in the face that had drawn blood, one day, in the Brasserie Zimmer, a blow from a man whom she gave herself the sly pleasure of refusing simply because he was low—and she had cried for help several times, though not without taking the time, before disappearing, to bleed all over the man's clothes—this story, when she was aimlessly telling it to me, early in the afternoon of October 13, almost managed to alienate me from her forever. I don't know what

sense of absolute irremediability her rather bantering
account of this horrible incident inspired in me, but
I wept a long time after hearing it, cried as though
I could no longer cry. I wept at the notion that I
shouldn't see Nadja again, not that I couldn't. Not
that I was angry at her for not concealing what was
now distressing me, indeed I was grateful for that,
but that she might one day reach this point, that—
who knows—such days might dawn again for her,
I didn't have the heart to imagine. At this moment
she was so touching, making no effort to oppose
my resolution, gaining from her tears, instead, the
strength to urge me to keep to it! While saying fare-
well to me, to Paris, she still couldn't keep from
adding in a low voice that it was impossible, but she
did nothing, then, for it to be more so. If it should
be so definitively, that would depend on me alone.

I have seen Nadja several times since, for me her
thought has become still clearer, and her expression
has gained in lightness, in originality, in depth. Perhaps, during the same period, the irreparable disaster
sweeping away a part of herself—and the most hu-
manly defined part—the disaster of which that day
gave me a notion, had gradually separated me from
her. Astonished as I continued to be by her behavior,
based as it was on the purest intuition alone and
ceaselessly relying on miracle, I was also increasingly
alarmed to feel that, when even I left her, she was

sucked back into the whirlwind of ordinary life continuing around her and eager to force her, among other concessions, to eat, to sleep. For some time I have tried to give her the means to do so, since, indeed, she expected them from me alone. But since on certain days she seemed to live only by my presence, without paying the slightest attention to my words or even—when she spoke to me about indifferent matters or said nothing—making the slightest concession to my own distress, I strongly doubt the influence I can have had over her, to help her to resolve such difficulties normally. It would be futile to multiply here instances of unusual happenings which apparently concern only the two of us and dispose me, for the most part, in favor of a certain finalism which might permit us to explain the particularity of any thing,* happenings, I say, of which Nadja and I have been the simultaneous witnesses or of which only one of us has been the witness. I no longer wish to remember, as the days go by, any but a few of her sentences, spoken or written spontaneously in my presence, sentences in which I best recapture the tone of her voice and whose resonance remains so great within me:

"With the end of my breath, which is the beginning of yours."

* Any notion of teleological justification in this area being, of course, rejected in advance.

"If you desired it, for you I would be nothing, or merely a footprint."

"The lion's claw embraces the vine's breast."

"Pink is better than black, but the two harmonize."

"Before the mystery. Man of stone, understand me."

"You are my master. I am only an atom respiring at the corner of your lips or expiring. I want to touch serenity with a finger wet with tears."

"Why this scale which wavered in the darkness of a hole full of coal pellets?"

"Not to weigh down one's thoughts with the weight of one's shoes."

"I knew everything, so hard have I tried to read in my streams of tears."

Nadja has invented a marvelous flower for me: "the Lovers' Flower." It is during a lunch in the country that this flower appeared to her and that I saw her trying—quite clumsily—to reproduce it. She comes back to it several times, afterwards, to improve the drawing and give each of the two pairs of eyes a different expression. It is essentially under this sign that the time we spent together should be placed, and it remains the graphic symbol which has given Nadja the key to all the rest. Several times she has tried to draw my portrait with my hair standing on end—as though sucked up by a high wind —like long flames. These flames also formed the

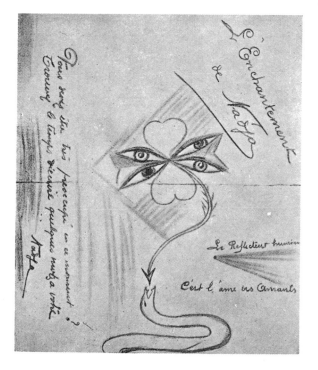

PLATE 29. "The Lovers' Flower"
(SEE PAGE 116)

PLATE 30. A symbolic portrait of the two of us
(SEE PAGE 121)

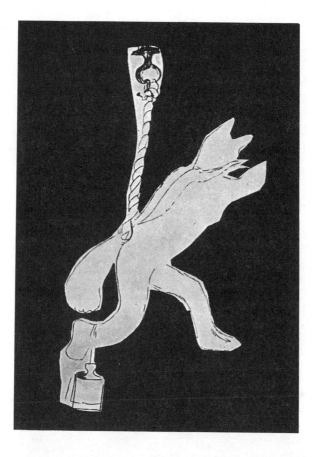

PLATE 31. "The Cat's Dream"

(SEE PAGE 121)

PLATE 32. So that the angle of the
head can be varied . . .

(SEE PAGE 121)

belly of an eagle whose heavy wings fell on either side of my head. After an inopportune remark I had made to her about one of the last, and the best, of these drawings, she unfortunately cut off the whole lower part, which was by far the richest in curious attributes. The drawing, dated November 18, 1926, consists of a symbolic portrait of the two of us: the siren, which is how she saw herself always from behind and from this angle, holds a scroll in her hand, the monster with gleaming eyes has the front of its body caught in a kind of eagle-head vase, filled with feathers representing ideas. "The Cat's Dream," showing the animal in a standing position trying to escape without realizing that it is held to the ground by a weight and suspended from a cord which is also the disproportionately enlarged wick of an over-turned lamp, remains the most obscure drawing for me. It is a cutout hastily made after a vision. There is enough cut out, but in two parts, so that the angle of the head can be varied, the whole consisting of a woman's face and a hand. "The Devil's Salute" is the result, like the "Cat's Dream," of a vision. The drawing in the shape of a helmet as well as another drawing called "A Cloudy Character" (too difficult to reproduce) are in another vein: they belong to that taste for searching in the folds of material, in knots of wood, in the cracks of old walls, for out-lines which are not there but which can readily be imagined. In the helmet-shaped drawing we can easily make out the Devil's face, a woman's head whose lips are being pecked at by a bird, the hair, torso, and tail of a siren seen from behind, an elephant's head, a sea lion, the face of another woman, a serpent, several more serpents, a heart, a kind of bull or buffalo head, the branches of the tree of good and evil, and some twenty other elements (rather slighted by reproduction) which make it into a true shield of Achilles. There is occasion to insist on the presence of two animal horns toward the upper right edge, a presence which Nadja herself did not explain, for they always appeared this way, as if what they were attached to necessarily and obstinately masked the siren's face (this is particularly noticeable in the drawing on the back of the postcard). A few days later, as a matter of fact, Nadja, visiting me at home, *recognized* these horns as those of a large Guinea mask which formerly belonged to Henri Matisse and which I have always loved and feared because of its monumental crest resembling a railroad signal, but which she could not see as she saw it *save from inside the library*. On the same occasion she recognized in a painting by Braque (*The Guitar Player*) the nail and the string, outside the central figure, which have always intrigued me; and in Chirico's triangular painting (*The Agonizing Journey* or *The Enigma of Fatality*, for the titles of this painter's

PLATE 33. Drawings by Nadja:
"Who is she?" "The Devil's Salute"
(SEE PAGE 121)

PLATE 34. A true shield of Achilles

(SEE PAGE 122)

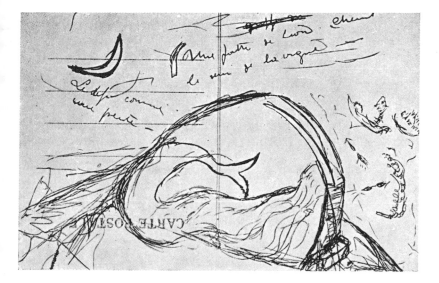

PLATE 35. On the back of the postcard
(SEE PAGE 122)

PLATE 36. "The Soul of the Wheat"
(a drawing by Nadja)

PLATE 37. The nail and the string, outside the central
figure, which have always intrigued me . . .

(SEE PAGE 122)

PLATE 38. *The Agonizing Journey* or
The Enigma of Fatality
(SEE PAGE 122)

work are disputed) the famous hand of fire. A con-
ical mask from New Britain, made of reeds and red
elder fiber, made her exclaim: "Goodness, Chimène!"
and a small statue of a seated Cacique looked more
threatening to her than the others; she offered a long
explanation of Max Ernst's extremely difficult painting *But Men Will Know Nothing About It* which
agreed in every particular with the detailed legend
on the back of the canvas; she decided that another
fetish, which I no longer own, was the god of
slander; another, from Easter Island, the first example of primitive art I ever possessed, said to her: "I
love you, I love you." Nadja has also represented herself many times with the features of Melusina, who
of all mythological personalities is the one she seems
to have felt closest to herself. I have even seen her
try to transfer this resemblance to real life, insisting
that her hairdresser spare no efforts to arrange her
hair in five distinct strands in order to leave a star
over her forehead. The strands must be coiled besides, to make ram's horns in front of her ears, the
spiral of such horns also being one of the motifs she
most frequently related to herself. She enjoyed imagining herself as a butterfly whose body consisted of a
Mazda (Nadja) bulb toward which rose a charmed
snake (and now I am invariably disturbed when I
pass the luminous Mazda sign on the main boulevards,
covering almost the entire façade of the former

Théâtre du Vaudeville where, in fact, two rams do confront one another in a rainbow light). But the last drawings, then unfinished, which Nadja showed me during the last visit I paid her, and which must have vanished in the torment that carried her away, evidenced an altogether different skill. (Before we met, she had never drawn at all.) In these, on a table, in front of an open book, a cigarette lying on an ashtray and insidiously releasing a serpent of smoke, a globe cut open to hold lilies, between the hands of a beautiful woman—everything was arranged to permit the descent of what she called the *human reflector*, kept off by forceps, and which she said was "the best of all."

. . . .

For some time, I had stopped understanding Nadja. Actually, perhaps we have never understood one another, at least about our way of dealing with the simple matters of existence. She had decided once and for all to take no account of them, to withdraw from the present moment, to make no differentiation between the trifling remarks which she happened to make and those others which meant so much to me, to ignore my momentary moods and my considerable difficulty in forgiving her her worst fits of abstraction. She had no hesitation, as I have said, about

PLATE 39. "Goodness, Chimène!"

(SEE PAGE 129)

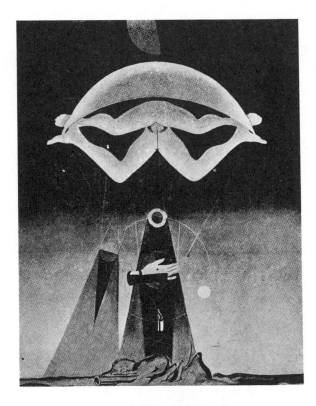

PLATE 40. *But Men Will Know Nothing About It*
(SEE PAGE 129)

PLATE 41. "I love you, I love you"
(SEE PAGE 129)

PLATE 42. The luminous Mazda sign on the boulevards
(SEE PAGE 129)

telling me the most unfortunate vicissitudes of her life, not omitting a single detail, occasionally succumbing to uncalled-for coquetries, forcing me to wait, brows knit, until she felt like proceeding to other exercises, for of course there was no question of her becoming *natural*. How many times, unable to endure it any longer, desperate to restore her to a true conception of her worth, I virtually fled from her presence hoping to find her, the next day, as she could be when she herself was not desperately blaming my strictness and seeking forgiveness. In these deplorable respects, however, it must be admitted that she spared me less and less, and that finally we could not avoid violent discussions, which she aggravated by attributing them to trivial causes which did not exist. Everything that permits us to live another's life without ever desiring to obtain more from him than he gives, so that it is quite enough to see him move or be still, speak or be silent, wake or sleep, no longer existed for me, had never existed: this was only too certain. It could scarcely be otherwise, considering the world which was Nadja's, where everything so rapidly assumed the appearance of a rise, a fall. But I am judging *a posteriori* and I merely speculate when I say it could not be otherwise. Whatever desire or even illusion I may have had to the contrary, perhaps I have not been adequate to what she offered me. But what was she offering me? It does not matter. Only love in the sense I understand it—mysterious, improbable, unique, bewildering, and *certain* love that can only be *foolproof*, might have permitted the fulfillment of a miracle.

I was told, several months ago, that Nadja was mad. After the eccentricities in which it seems she had indulged herself in the hallways of her hotel, she had had to be committed to the Vaucluse sanitarium. Others will provide their useless epilogues on this fact, which they will inevitably interpret as the fatal result of all that has gone before. The more enlightened will certainly stigmatize the role which must be attributed, in what I have related of Nadja, to ideas already frenzied and will perhaps set a terribly decisive value to my role in her life, a role favorable, in practice, to the development of such ideas. As for those who say "oh, well," or "you see," "I thought so all along," "under these conditions," for all such imbeciles, it goes without saying that I prefer to leave them in peace. The essential thing is that I do not suppose there can be much difference for Nadja between the inside of a sanitarium and the outside. There must, unfortunately, be a difference all the same, on account of the grating sound of a key turning in a lock, or the wretched view of the garden, the cheek of the people who question you when you want to be left alone, like

PHOTO: HENRI MANUEL

PLATE 43. Like Professor Claude at Sainte-Anne . . .

(SEE PAGE 139)

Professor Claude at Sainte-Anne, with his dunce's forehead and that stubborn expression on his face ("You're being persecuted, aren't you?"—"No, Monsieur."—"He's lying, last week he told me he was being persecuted" or even: "You hear voices, do you? Well, are they voices like mine?"—"No, Monsieur."—"You see, he has auditory hallucinations," etc.) and on account of the uniform—neither more nor less wretched than all uniforms, and on account of the effort necessary to adapt oneself to any milieu, for it is, after all, a *milieu* and, as such, it requires a certain degree of adaptation. Unless you have been inside a sanitarium you do not know that madmen are *made* there, just as criminals are made in our reformatories. Is there anything more detestable than these systems of so-called social conservation which, for a peccadillo, some initial and exterior rejection of respectability or common sense, hurl an individual among others whose association can only be harmful to him and, above all, systematically deprive him of relations with everyone whose moral or practical sense is more firmly established than his own? The newspapers tell us that at the latest international congress of psychiatry, the delegates were unanimous in castigating the persistent popular notion that it should be as difficult to leave asylums today as it once was to leave a convent; we discover that people have been committed for life who have never had any reason, or who have no further reason, to be in institutions at all; we are informed that public safety is not so generally at stake as we have been led to believe. Yet each of these psychiatrists protested against one or two instances of release to active life, furnishing certain examples of catastrophes occasioned by patients' ill-advised or premature return to liberty. Their responsibility being always more or less involved in such matters, psychiatrists let it be understood that in doubtful cases they prefer to abstain. In this form, however, I regard the question as badly put. The atmosphere of sanitariums is such that it cannot fail to exercise the most debilitating, the most pernicious influence upon those it shelters, and this in the very direction their initial debilitation has led them; further complicated by the fact that any demand, any protest, any movement of resistance merely raises charges of insociability (for, however paradoxically, even in this realm one must be sociable), serves only to charge you with a new symptom, by its nature not only prevents your cure but even keeps your state from remaining stable and rapidly deteriorates it instead. Hence those tragically swift evolutions we can follow in the sanitariums and which, quite often, are not those of one illness alone. There is occasion to denounce, with regard to mental illness, the *processus* of this virtually fatal passage from acute crises to chronic illness.

Given the extraordinary and retarded infancy of psychiatry, we simply cannot speak of cures effected under such conditions. I suppose that the most conscientious psychiatrist is not even concerned with cures. Granted that there is no longer such a thing as arbitrary confinement in the sense in which we customarily understand it, since a patent and objectively ascertainable fact, of abnormal character and committed in the highest degree against public interest, is the cause of these detentions, which are a thousand times more horrible than the others. But as I see it, all confinements are arbitrary. I still cannot see why a human being should be deprived of freedom. They shut up Sade, they shut up Nietzsche; they shut up Baudelaire. The method which consists in surprising you by night, forcing you into a strait jacket or capturing you in any other way, is no better than that of the policeman who slips a revolver into your pocket. I know that if I were mad, after several days of confinement I should take advantage of any lapses in my madness to murder anyone, preferably a doctor, who came near me. At least this would permit me, like the violent, to be confined in solitary. Perhaps they'd leave me alone.

My general contempt for psychiatry, its rituals and its works, is reason enough for my not yet having dared investigate what has become of Nadja. I have indicated my pessimism as to her fate, as to that of several others of her kind. Treated in a private rest-home with all the consideration granted the rich, suffering no contacts which might be harmful to her, but instead comforted at propitious moments by friendly presences, her preferences gratified as much as possible, gradually restored to an acceptable sense of reality—which would have necessitated the avoidance of all harsh treatment and an effort to induce her to recognize voluntarily the origin of her difficulties—I may be making a rash statement, yet everything leads me to believe that she would have recovered from her wretched state. But Nadja was poor, which in our time is enough to condemn her, once she decided not to behave entirely according to the imbecile code of good sense and good manners. She was also alone: "At times, it is terrible to be so alone. I have no friends but you," she said to my wife on the telephone, the last time. She was, finally, strong, and extremely weak, as one can be, in that idea she had always had but in which I had only too warmly encouraged her, which I had only too readily aided her in giving supremacy over all the rest: the idea that freedom, acquired here on earth at the price of a thousand—and the most difficult—renunciations, must be enjoyed as unrestrictedly as it is granted, without pragmatic considerations of any sort, and this because human emancipation—conceived finally in its simplest revolutionary form, which is no less than human emancipation in *every respect*, by which I mean, *according to the means at every man's disposal*—remains the only cause worth serving. Nadja was born to serve it, if only by demonstrating that around himself each individual must foment a private conspiracy, which exists not only in his imagination—of which it would be best, from the standpoint of knowledge alone, to take account —but also—and much more dangerously—by thrusting one's head, then an arm, out of the jail—thus shattered—of logic, that is, out of the most hateful of prisons. It is from this last enterprise, perhaps, that I should have restrained her, but first of all I should have had to become conscious of the danger she ran. Yet I never supposed she could lose or might have already lost that minimal common sense which permits my friends and myself, for instance to *stand up* when a flag goes past, confining ourselves to not saluting it; so we do not side with whatever we feel sympathetic to on every occasion, nor permit ourselves the unparalleled joy of committing some splendid sacrilege, etc. . . . My judgment may appear questionable, but I confess it did not seem exorbitant to me, among other things, when Nadja happened to show me a letter signed "Henri Becque" in which the latter gave her advice. If this advice was disadvantageous to me, I merely replied: "It is impossible that Becque, who was an intelligent man, said anything like that to you." But I understood perfectly, since she was attracted by Becque's bust in the Place Villiers, and because she liked the expression on his face, that she should insist—and on certain subjects successfully—on having his advice. Surely this is no more unreasonable than asking some saint or divinity what one should do. Nor could Nadja's letters, which I read the same way I read all kinds of surrealist texts—with the same eye—show me anything alarming. I shall add, in my defense, only a few words. The well-known lack of frontiers between *non-madness* and madness does not induce me to accord a different value to the perceptions and ideas which are the result of one or the other. There are sophisms infinitely more significant and far-reaching than the most indisputable truths: to call them into question as sophisms, it must be admitted that they have done more than anything else to make me hurl at myself or at anyone who comes to meet me, the forever pathetic cry of "Who goes there? Is it you, Nadja? Is it true that the beyond, that everything beyond is here in this life? I can't hear you. Who goes there? Is it only me? Is it myself?"

I envy (in a manner of speaking) any man who has the time to prepare something like a book and who, having reached the end, finds the means to be interested in its fate or in the fate which, after all, it creates for him. If only he would let me believe that on the way at least one true occasion to give it up presented itself! He would have disregarded the chance, and we might hope he would do us the honor of saying why. What I might be tempted to undertake in the long run will all too

certainly make me unworthy of life as I prefer it
and as it offers itself: a life *out of the running*. The
sudden intervals between words in even a printed
sentence, the line which as we speak, we draw beneath a certain number of propositions whose total
is out of the question, the complete elision of events
which, from one day to the next or to another, quite
upsets the data of a problem we thought we could
solve, the vague emotional coefficient applied to and
removed from the remotest ideas we dream of pro-
ducing, as well as our most concrete recollections,
as time goes by—all these function so that I no
longer have the heart to consider anything but the
interval separating these last lines from those which,
leafing through this book, would seem to have come
to an end a few pages back.* A short interval—negli-
gible for a hurried reader and even for any other,
but, I must say, enormous and priceless for me. How
can I make myself understood? If I were to reread

* Thus I remarked, while idling on the quay of the
Vieux-Port in Marseille, shortly before sunset, a curiously
scrupulous painter struggling with skill and speed on his
canvas against the fading light. The spot of color corresponding to the sun gradually descended with the sun. Finally, nothing remained. The painter suddenly discovered
he was far behind: he obliterated the red from a wall,
painted over one or two last gleams lingering on the water.
His painting, finished for himself, for me the most *unfinished* thing possible, looked very sad and very beautiful.

PHOTO: HENRI MANUEL

PLATE 44. I envy (in a manner of speaking) any man
who has the time to prepare something like a book . . .

(SEE PAGE 147)

this story, with the patient and somehow disinterested eye I would be sure to have, I hardly know, to be faithful to my present sense of myself, what I would leave standing. I do not insist upon knowing. I prefer thinking that from the end of August, the date of her first appearance, to the end of December, when this story, finding me bent beneath a burden of infinitely greater emotion, detaches itself from me and begins to alarm me, I have lived badly or well—as one can—in the hopes she left me, believe me if you will, of the realization, yes of the total realization of such hopes. This is why the voice that speaks in them still seems to me to deserve a hearing, in human terms; this is why I do not repudiate a few rare accents which I have set there. When Nadja, Nadja's person, is so far. . . . As are several others. And when, brought to me—who knows, already taken back—by the Marvel, the Marvel in which, from the first page of this book to the last, my faith will certainly not have changed, there chimes in my ear a name which is no longer hers.

. . . .

I have begun by going back to look at several of the places to which this narrative happens to lead; I wanted in fact—with some of the people and some of the objects—to provide a photographic image of them taken at the special angle from which I myself had looked at them. On this occasion, I realized that most of the places more or less resisted my venture, so that, as I see it, the illustrated part of *Nadja* is quite inadequate: Becque surrounded by sinister palings, the management of the Théâtre Moderne on its guard, Porville dead and disillusioning as any French city, the disappearance of almost everything relating to *The Grip of the Octopus* and, above all —for I regarded it as essential, although it has not been otherwise referred to in this book—the impossibility of obtaining permission to photograph an adorable wax-work figure in the Musée Grevin, on the left, between the hall of modern political celebrities and the hall at the rear of which, behind a curtain, is shown "an evening at the theater": it is a woman fastening her garter in the shadows, and is the only statue I know of with eyes, the eyes of provocation, etc.* While the Boulevard Bonne-Nouvelle, after having—unfortunately during my

---

* I had not been granted the realization, until today, of all that in Nadja's attitude toward me derives from the application of a more or less conscious principle of total subversion, of which I will give only this example: one evening, when I was driving a car along the road from Versailles to Paris, the woman sitting beside me (who was Nadja, but who might have been anyone else, after all, or even *someone else*) pressed her foot down on mine on the accelerator, tried to cover my eyes with her hands in the oblivion of an interminable kiss, desiring to extinguish us, doubtless forever, save to each other, so that we

absence from Paris, in the course of the magnificent days of riot called "Sacco-Vanzetti"—seemed to come up to my expectation, after even revealing itself as one of the major strategic points I am looking for in matters of chaos, points which I persist in believing obscurely provided for me, as for anyone who chooses to yield to inexplicable entreaties, provided the most absolute sense of love or revolution are at stake and that this, naturally, involved the negation of everything else; while the Boulevard

---

should collide at full speed with the splendid trees along the road. What a test of life, indeed! Unnecessary to add that I did not yield to this desire. It is clear how I felt—how, so far as I know, I have almost always felt—about Nadja. I am no less grateful to her for revealing to me, in such an overpowering way, what a common recognition of love would have committed us to at that moment. I feel less and less capable of resisting such a temptation *in every case*. I can do no less than offer thanks in this last recollection, to the woman who has made me understand its virtual necessity. It is by an extreme capacity for defiance that certain unusual people who have everything to hope and everything to fear from one another will always recognize one another. In imagination, at least, I often find myself, eyes blindfolded, back at the wheel of that wild car. Just as I am sure of finding *refuge* among my friends when my head is worth its weight in gold and they run an enormous risk in taking me in—they are indebted to me only for this tragic trust I place in them—so, as regards love, the only question that exists for me is to resume, under all the requisite conditions, that nocturnal ride.

Bonne-Nouvelle, the façades of its movie-theaters re-
painted, has subsequently become immobilized for
me, as if the Porte Saint-Denis had just closed, I
have seen reborn and die again the Théâtre des Deux-
Masques, which was once nothing more than the
Théâtre du Masque and which, still in the Rue Fontaine, was no more than a short walk from my house.
Etc. It's queer, as that abominable gardener used to
say. But that is the way of the world, isn't it, the
outer world, that is—a matter of sleep-walking. That
is the kind of weather it is, I wouldn't put a dog out
in weather like this.

It is not for me to ponder what is happening to
the "shape of a city," even of the true city distracted
and abstracted from the one I live in by the force
of an element which is to my mind what air is supposed to be to life. Without regret, at this moment
I see it change and even disappear. It slides, it burns,
it sinks into the shudder of weeds along its barri-
cades, into the dream of curtains in its bedrooms,
where a man and woman indifferently continue making love. I leave this sketch of a mental landscape
whose limits discourage me, despite its remarkable
extension toward Avignon, where the Palace of the
Popes has not suffered from winter nights and driving rain, where an old bridge has finally succumbed
beneath a nursery tune, where a marvelous and un-
betrayable hand has shown me, not long enough

ago, a huge sky-blue street sign bearing these words: THE DAWNS. Despite this extension and all the others which help me plant a star at the very heart of the *finite*. I predict, and this is no better substantiated than what I have already predicted. Yet if I must wait, if I must be sure, if I must take precautions, if I must give the devil his due, and only his due, I shall refuse, and absolutely. May the great living and echoing unconsciousness which inspires my only conclusive acts in any sense I always believe in, dispose forever of all that is myself. I gladly renounce any possibility of taking back what here, again, I bestow upon it. Once more I want to recognize and rely on it alone and virtually at my leisure wander along its immense piers, staring at some shining dot I know is in my own eye and which saves me all collision with its night freight.

I was recently told a story that was so stupid, so melancholy, and so moving: a man comes into a hotel one day and asks to rent a room. He is shown up to number 35. As he comes down a few minutes later and leaves the key at the desk, he says: "Excuse me, I have no memory at all. If you please, each time I come in, I'll tell you my name: Monsieur Delouit.* And each time you'll tell me the number of my room."—"Very well, Monsieur." Soon afterwards, he returns, and as he passes the desk says: "Monsieur

* I do not know how this name is spelled.

Delouit." — "Number 35, Monsieur." — "Thank you." A minute later, a man extraordinarily upset, his clothes covered with mud, bleeding, his face almost not a face at all, appears at the desk: "Monsieur Delouit." "What do you mean, Monsieur Delouit? Don't try to put one over on us! Monsieur Delouit has just gone upstairs!"—"I'm sorry, it's me . . . I've just fallen out of the window. What's the number of my room, please?"

.   .   .   .

That is the story that I too yielded to the desire to tell *you*, when I scarcely knew you—you who can no longer remember but who, as if by chance, knowing of the beginning of this book, have intervened so opportunely, so violently, and so effectively, doubtless to remind me that I wanted it to be "ajar, like a door" and that through this door I should probably never see anyone come in but you —come in and go out but you. You who from all I have said here will have received only a little rain on your hand raised toward "THE DAWNS." You who make me so greatly regret writing that absurd and undeniable sentence about love, love "that must be foolproof." You who, for all those who hear me must be not an entity but a woman, you who are nothing so much as a woman, despite all that has been levied upon me and upon me in you to make into a Chimera. You who do so wonderfully all that you do and whose splendid reasons, not bounded for me in unreason, dazzle and fall inexorably as thunderbolts. You, the most vital of beings, who seem to have been put in my path only so I may feel in all its rigor the strength of what is not felt in you. You who know evil only by hearsay. You, indeed, ideally beautiful. You whom everything identifies with daybreak and whom, for this very reason, I may not see again. . . .

Without you what shall I do with my abiding love of genius, in whose name I have at least been able to attempt a few acknowledgments here and there? I flatter myself I know where genius is, almost what it consists of, and I held it capable of conciliating all the other great passions with itself. I believe blindly in your genius. Reluctantly, sadly, I withdraw this word, if it shocks you. But in that case, I prefer to banish it altogether. Genius . . . what could I still expect from the few possible *intercessors* who have appeared to me under this sign, and which, at your side, I have ceased to possess!

Without doing it on purpose, you have taken the place of the forms most familiar to me, as well as of several figures of my foreboding. Nadja was one of these last, and it is just that you should have hidden her from me.

All I know is that this substitution of persons stops with you, because nothing can be substituted for you, and because for me it was for all eternity that this succession of terrible or charming enigmas was to come to an end at your feet.

You are not an enigma for me.

I say that you have turned me from enigmas forever.

Since you exist, as you alone know how to *exist*, it was perhaps not so necessary that this book should exist. I have decided to write it nevertheless, in memory of the conclusion I wanted to give it before knowing you and which your explosion into my life has not rendered vain. This conclusion has its true meaning and all its strength only through your intercession.

It smiles at me as sometimes you have smiled at me, behind great thickets of tears. "It's still love," you used to say, and more unjustly, you would also say: "All or nothing."

I shall never dispute this rule, with which passion has armed itself. At the most I might question it as to the nature of this "all"—whether, in this regard, it must to be unable to hear me in order to be passion. As for its *various movements*, even insofar as I am their victim—and whether or not it can ever deprive me of speech, suppress my right to exist —how could they divorce me from the pride of knowing passion itself, from the absolute humility I should feel before it and before it alone? I shall not appeal its most mysterious, its harshest decrees. It would be as if I were to try to stop the course of the world, by virtue of some illusory power passion has over it. Or to deny that "each man hopes and believes he is better than the world which is his, but the man who *is* better merely expresses this same world better than the others." *

. . . .

A certain attitude necessarily follows with regard to beauty, which has obviously never been envisaged here save for emotional purposes. In no way static, that is, enclosed in Baudelaire's "dream of stone," lost for man in the shadow of those Odalisques, in the depth of those tragedies which claim to girdle only a single day, scarcely less dynamic—that is, subject to that wild gallop which can lead only to another wild gallop—that is, more frenzied than a snowflake in a blizzard—that is, resolved, for fear of being fettered, never to be embraced at all: neither dynamic nor static, I see beauty as I have seen you. As I have seen what, at the given hour and for a given time which I hope and with all my soul believe may recur, granted you to me. Beauty is like

* Hegel.

a train that ceaselessly roars out of the Gare de Lyon and which I know will never leave, which has not left. It consists of jolts and shocks, many of which do not have much importance, but which we know are destined to produce one *Shock*, which does. Which has all the importance I do not want to arrogate to myself. In every domain the mind appropriates certain rights which it does not possess. Beauty, neither static nor dynamic. The human heart, beautiful as a seismograph. Royalty of silence. . . . A morning paper will always be adequate to give me my news:

> X . . . , December 26.—The radio operator on the *Ile du Sable* has received a fragment of a message sent Sunday evening at such and such an hour by the. . . . The message said, in particular: "There is something which is not working" but failed to indicate the position of the plane at this moment, and due to extremely bad atmospheric conditions and static, the operator was unable to understand any further sentence, nor to make communication again.
>
> The message was transmitted on a wave length of 625 meters; moreover given the strength of the reception, the operator states he can localize the plane within a radius of 50 miles around the *Ile du Sable*.

Beauty will be CONVULSIVE or will not be at all.